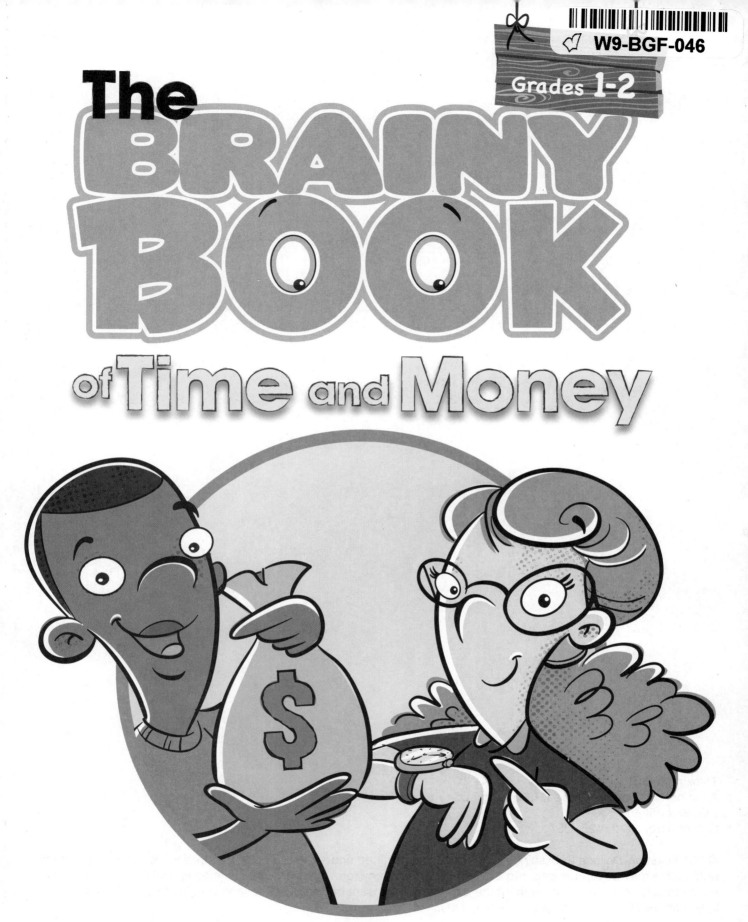

Grades 1-2

The BRAINY BOOK of Time and Money

Thinking Kids™
An imprint of Carson-Dellosa Publishing LLC
P.O. Box 35665
Greensboro, NC 27425 USA

Thinking Kids™
An imprint of Carson-Dellosa Publishing LLC
P.O. Box 35665
Greensboro, NC 27425 USA

Printed in the USA • All rights reserved.   ISBN 978-1-4838-1328-8
01-113157811

Table of Contents

Table of Contents

Analog Clocks: Introduction

What is the best way to tell what time it is? A clock!

There are all kinds of clocks. Circle the ones you have seen.

Analog Clocks: Identifying Parts

A clock can tell you what time it is.
A clock has different parts.

Read and trace each part of the clock.

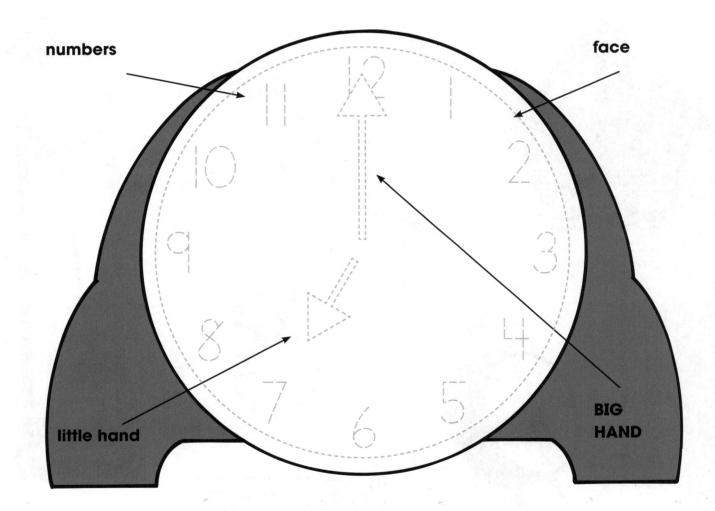

numbers

face

little hand

BIG
HAND

The **BIG HAND** is on **12**.
The **little hand tells the hour.**

A clock face has numbers.

Trace the numbers on the clock.

Name _____

Write the numbers on the clock face.
Draw the **BIG HAND** to **12**.
Draw the **little hand** to **5**.

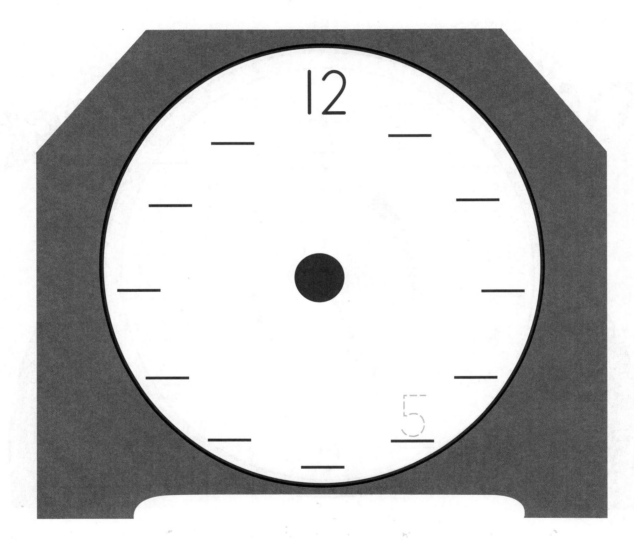

What time is it? _____ o'clock

Writing the Time

An **hour** is **sixty minutes** long.

It takes an **hour** for the **BIG HAND** to go around the clock.

When the **BIG HAND** is on **12**, and the **little hand** points to a number, that is **the hour**!

The **BIG HAND** is on the **12**. Color it red.
The **little hand** is on the **8**. Color it blue.

The BIG HAND is on _____.
The little hand is on _____.

It is _____ o'clock

Writing the Time

Color the **little hand** red. Fill in the blanks.

The BIG HAND is on _____.
The little hand is on _____.
It is _____ o'clock.

The BIG HAND is on _____.
The little hand is on _____.
It is _____ o'clock.

The BIG HAND is on _____.
The little hand is on _____.
It is _____ o'clock.

The BIG HAND is on _____.
The little hand is on _____.
It is _____ o'clock.

Name _____

If the **BIG HAND** is on 12, it is easy to tell the time. Look and see the hour.

Trace the **little hand** to make the hour **10 o'clock**.

The BIG HAND is on _____.
The little hand is on _____.
It is _____ o'clock.

Drawing the Hour Hand

Draw the **little hour hand** on each clock.

8 o'clock

1 o'clock

7 o'clock

Circling the Hour Hand

Circle the **little hour hand** on each clock. What time is it? Write the time below.

_____ o'clock

_____ o'clock

_____ o'clock

_____ o'clock

_____ o'clock

_____ o'clock

Practice

Draw the **little hour hand** on each clock.

8 o'clock

4 o'clock

2 o'clock

6 o'clock

11 o'clock

3 o'clock

1 o'clock

5 o'clock

7 o'clock

Practice

What is the time?

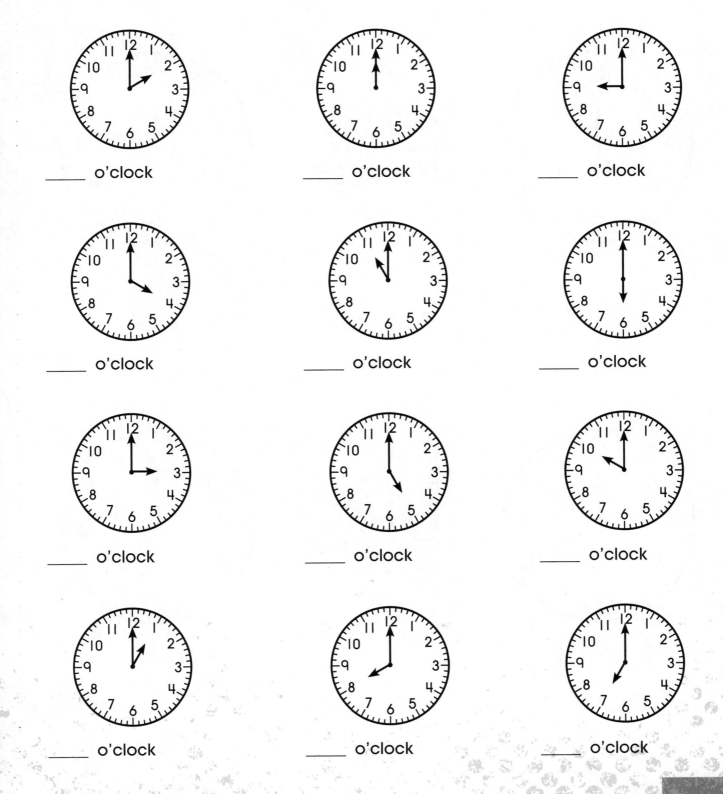

_____ o'clock   _____ o'clock   _____ o'clock

_____ o'clock   _____ o'clock   _____ o'clock

_____ o'clock   _____ o'clock   _____ o'clock

_____ o'clock   _____ o'clock   _____ o'clock

Writing the Time: One Hour Later

Write the original time and **1 hour later**.

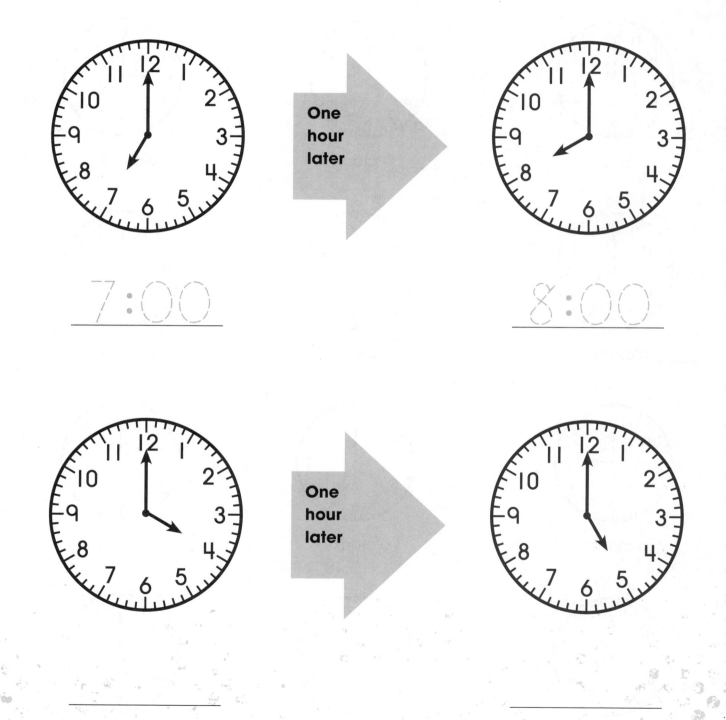

One hour later

7:00   8:00

One hour later

_____   _____

Writing the Time: One Hour Later

Place the hands on the clocks to show **I hour later**. Write the times.

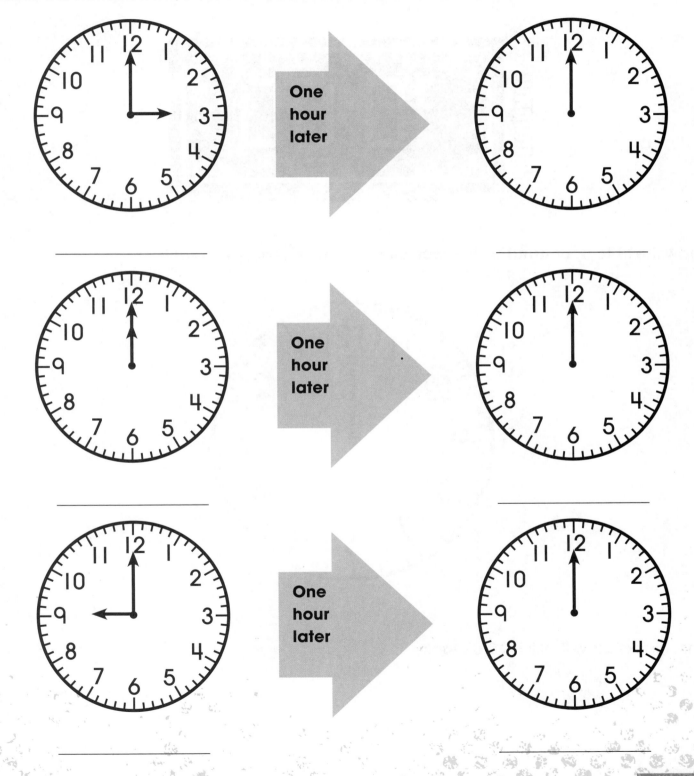

Digital Clocks: Introduction

A digital clock tells time with numbers. First, it tells the hour, then the minutes.

Draw the **little hour hand** on this face clock below to read **10 o'clock**.

Both clocks show that it is **10 o'clock**.

Matching Digital and Analog Clocks

Trace the time on the **digital clocks**.

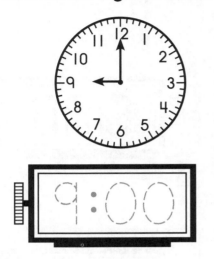

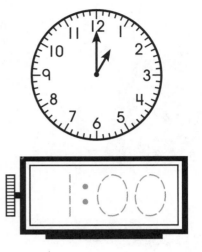

Match the clocks.

Matching Digital and Analog Clocks

Match these digital and analog clocks.

Digital Clocks

Write the time on the digital clocks.

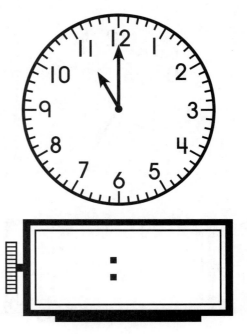

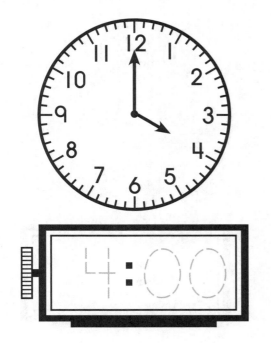

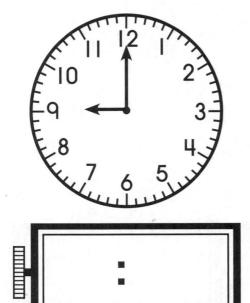

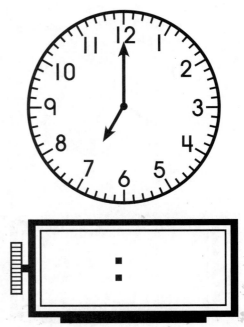

Digital Clocks

Write the time on the digital clocks.

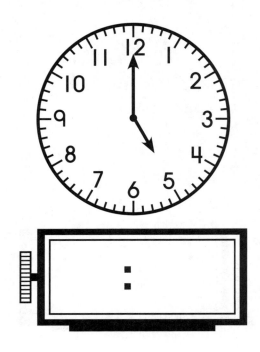

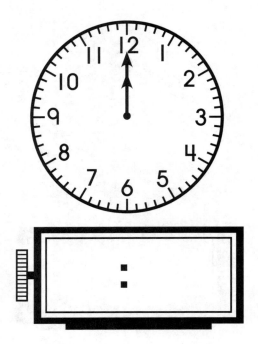

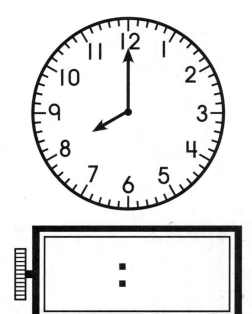

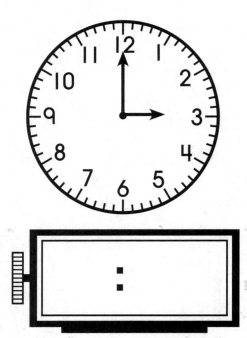

Brainy Book of Time and Money

Look at the digital clock. Say the time. Draw the **little hour hand** on each analog clock.

Drawing the Hour Hand: Matching Digital and Analog Clocks

Look at the digital clock. Say the time. Draw the **little hour hand** on each analog clock.

Time Two Ways

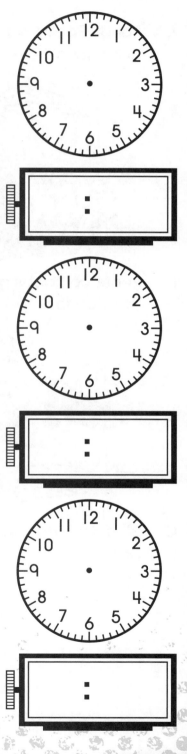

Show each time **two ways**. Draw the hands on each analog clock. Write the time on each digital clock.

A. Bessie Bear gets up at **6 o'clock**.

B. Bernie Bear eats breakfast at **7 o'clock**.

C. What time do you get up on school mornings? Draw it here!

Time Two Ways

Show each time **two ways**. Draw the hands on each analog clock. Write the time on each digital clock.

A.   Randy Rabbit leaves for school
at **8 o'clock**.

B.   Rebecca Rabbit goes out to recess
at **10 o'clock**.

C.   What time do you go out for recess?
Draw it here!

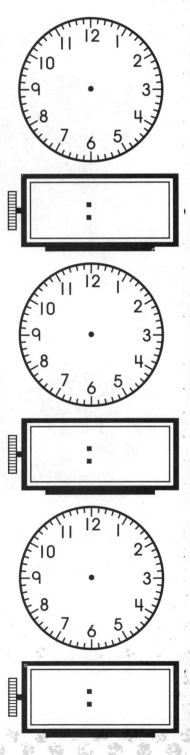

Time Stories

Read each story. Draw the hands on each analog clock.

A. At **11:00**, Mouse starts to cook. Yum-yum! Cheese soup is good.

B. At **12 o'clock**, Mouse sets the table. Uh-oh! He drops a spoon.

C. At **7:00**, Mouse reads a book. What a funny story!

D. Time for bed. It is **9 o'clock**, and Mouse is sleepy.

Time Stories

Read each story. Draw the hands on each analog clock.

A. Rabbit is hungry. It is **6 o'clock**—time for supper and some carrot stew.

B. At **8:00**, Rabbit washes the dishes. Scrub, scrub, the pot is sticky.

C. Rabbit works in his garden. It is **4 o'clock**, and he is picking lettuce.

D. At **5:00**, Rabbit makes a lettuce salad. What a tasty meal.

Time to the Half-Hour: Introduction

This clock face shows the time gone by since 8 o'clock.

Thirty minutes or **half an hour** has gone by.

There are 3 easy ways to say time to the half-hour.
We say **eight thirty**, **thirty past eight** or **half past eight**.

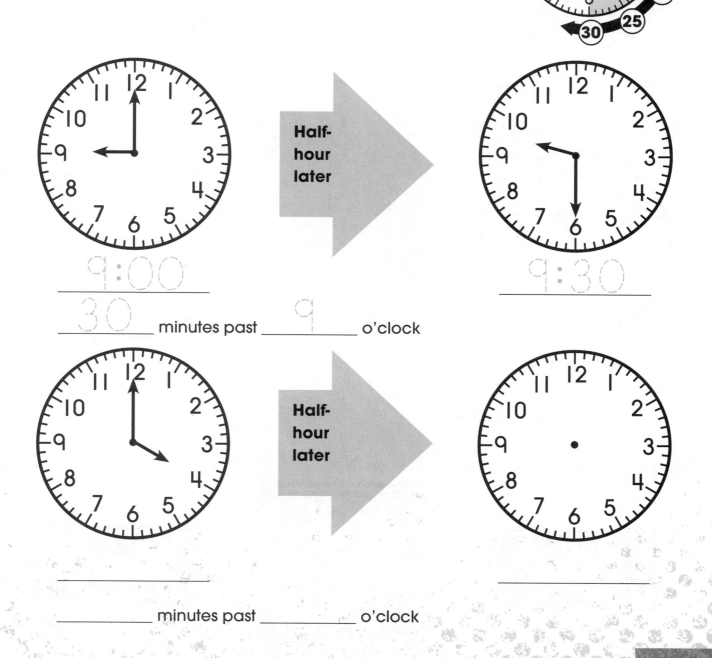

9:00

9:30

_____30_____ minutes past _____9_____ o'clock

_____ minutes past _____ o'clock

Writing Time on the Half-Hour

Half-hour later

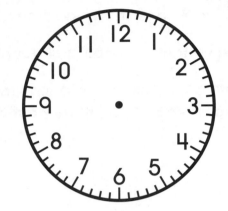

_____

_____ minutes past _____ o'clock

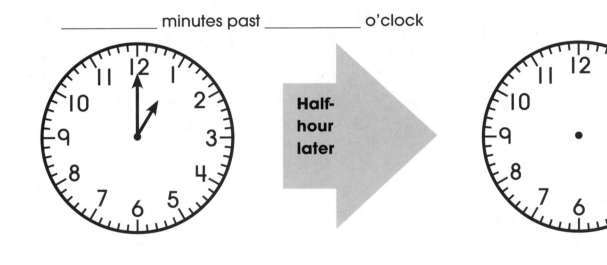

_____ minutes past _____ o'clock

What is your dinner time? Circle the time you eat.

Writing Time on the Half-Hour

What time is it?

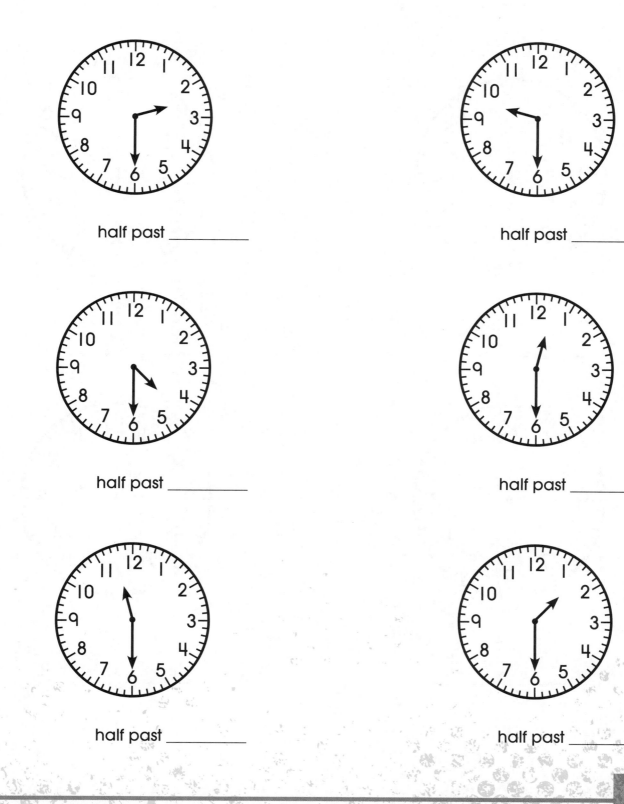

half past _____

half past _____

half past _____

half past _____

half past _____

half past _____

Writing Time on the Half-Hour

Trace the **BIG MINUTE HAND** green. Trace the **little hour hand** yellow. Write the time on the line.

_____

_____

These digital numbers got lost. Put them in the right clocks on this page and page 34.

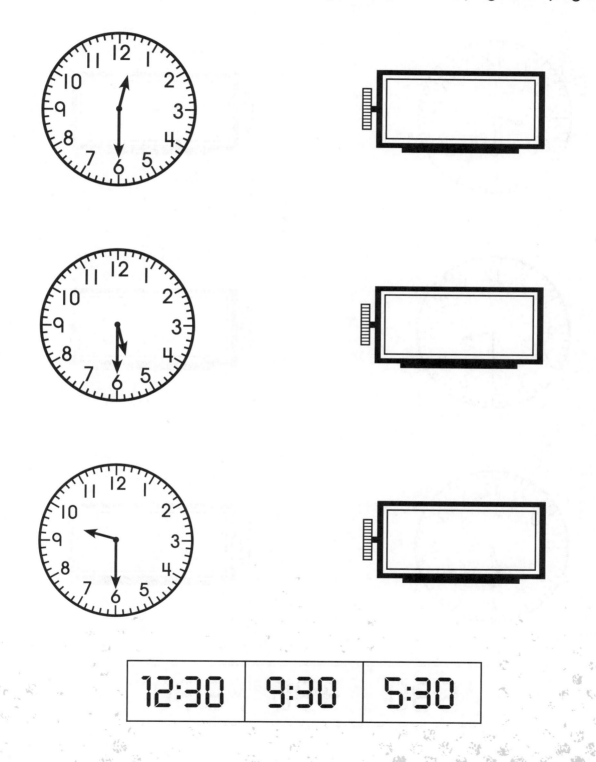

| 12:30 | 9:30 | 5:30 |

Matching Digital and Analog Clocks

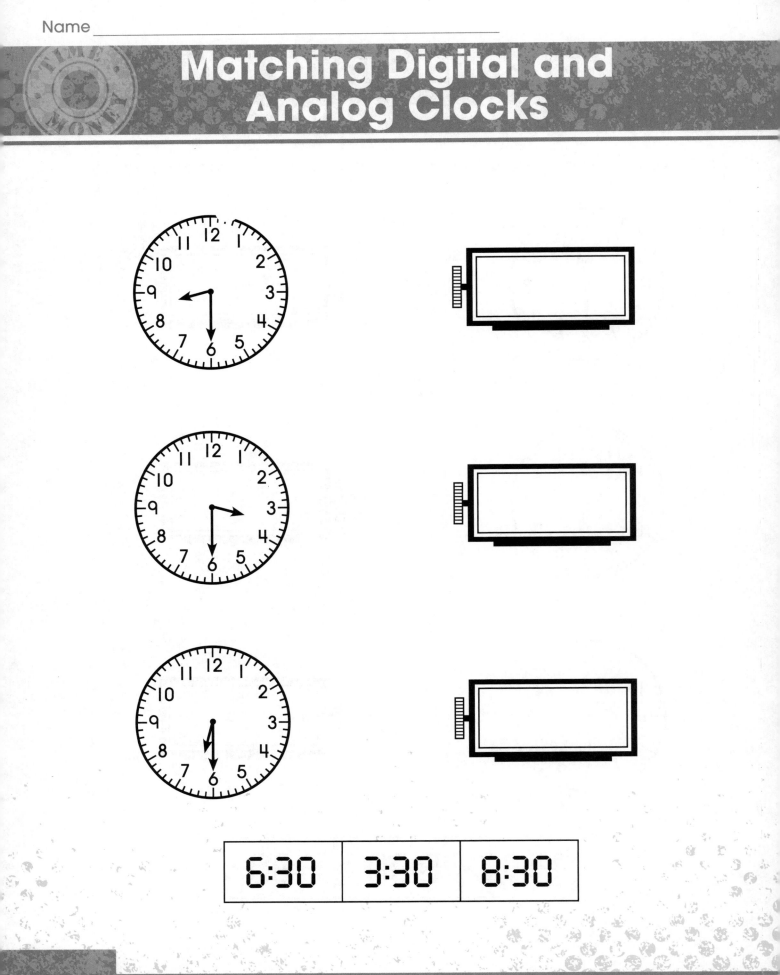

| 6:30 | 3:30 | 8:30 |

Name _____

Say the time. Draw the **little hour hand** on each clock.

Drawing the Hour Hand

Say the time. Draw the **little hour hand** on each clock.

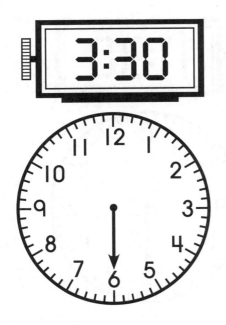

Telling Time: Hour and Half-Hour

Draw a line from the clock to the correct time.

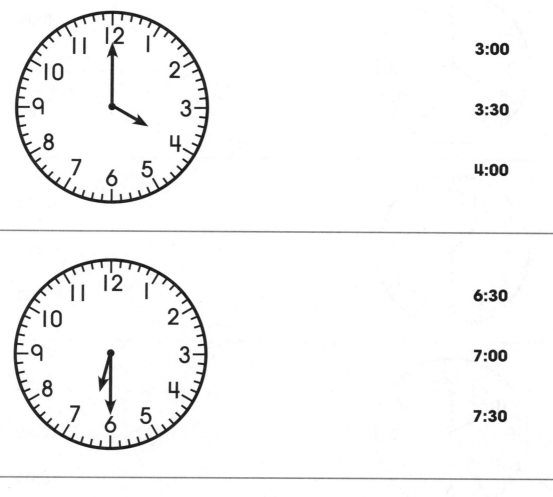

3:00

3:30

4:00

6:30

7:00

7:30

4:00

5:00

6:00

Telling Time: Hour and Half-Hour

Draw a line from the clock to the correct time.

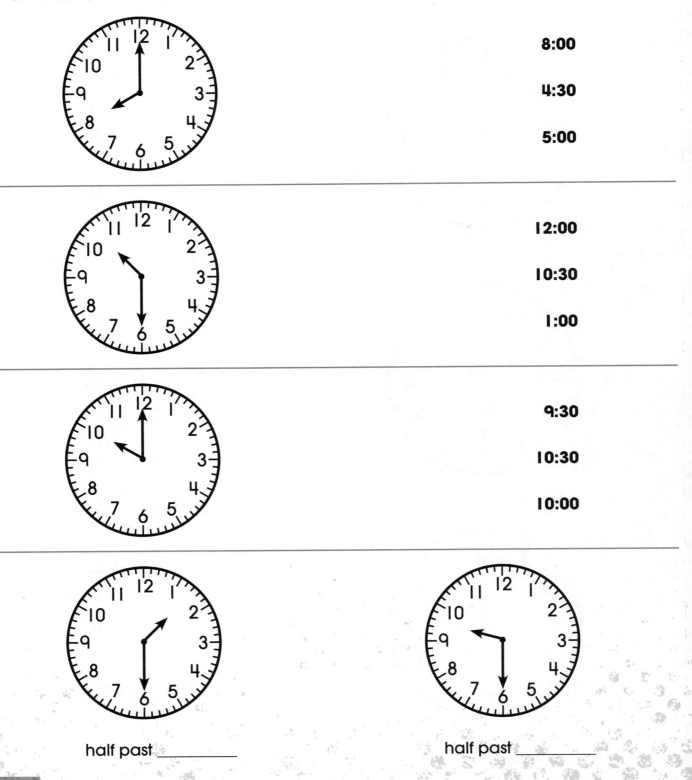

8:00

4:30

5:00

12:00

10:30

1:00

9:30

10:30

10:00

half past _____

half past _____

Writing the Time: Practice

What time is it?

3:00

Writing the Time: Practice

Draw the hands on the sock clocks.

1:30

7:00

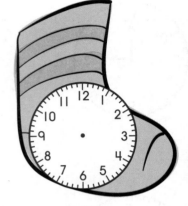

4:30

10:00

3:30

9:30

4:30

2:30

Matching Digital and Analog Clocks

Match each clock to the correct time.

Time Stories

Read each story. Draw the hands on each clock face.

A.   Hop, hop. It is **10:30**, and Frog is going to the market.

B.   At **11:30**, Frog heads home. She has a basket of tasty treats.

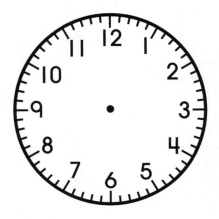

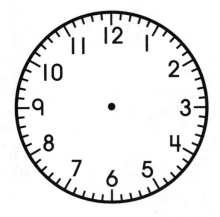

C.   At **4:30**, Frog is making a cake. The little frogs will eat it.

D.   By **7:30**, Frog's cake is all gone. My, that was good!

Time Stories

Read each story. Draw the hands on each clock face.

A. It is **5:30**, and the sun is coming up. Bird is ready for the day.

B. At **6:30**, Bird is looking for breakfast. Watch out worms!

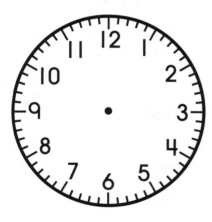

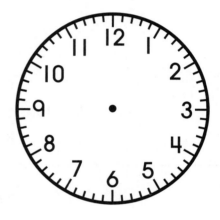

C. Bird is resting after breakfast. It is **9:30** and almost time for flying practice.

D. At **12:30**, Bird naps before lunch. Flying is hard work!

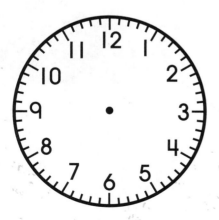

Can you tell how much time has passed?

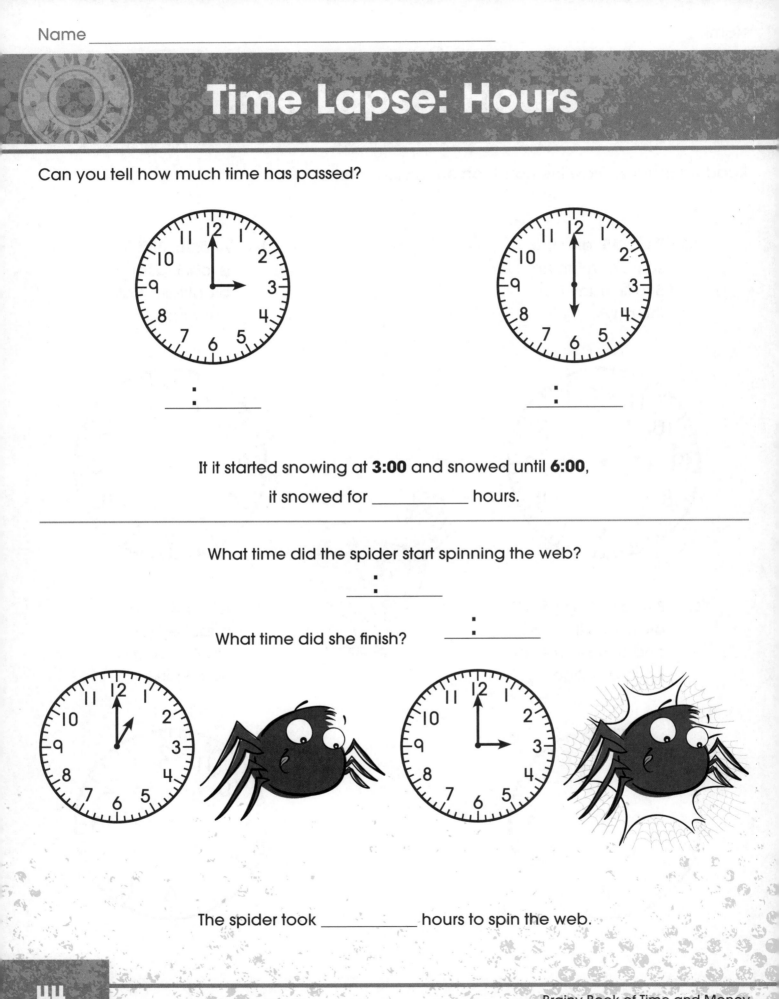

___ : ___   ___ : ___

It it started snowing at **3:00** and snowed until **6:00**,

it snowed for _____ hours.

What time did the spider start spinning the web?

___ : ___

What time did she finish?   ___ : ___

The spider took _____ hours to spin the web.

Time Lapse: Hours

Dad went to the grocery store.

_____ : _____   _____ : _____

Dad took _____ hour to buy groceries.

The teacher taught math class.

_____ : _____   _____ : _____

Math lasted _____ hour.

Write how much later.

_____ hours

Drawing the Hour Hand: A Half-Hour Later

Draw the hands on each clock face.

A. At **7:00**, Carlos turns on the TV.

What time is it one half-hour later?

B. At **4:00**, we all jump in the car.

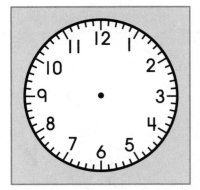

What time is it one half-hour later?

C. At **12:00**, Julio and Nathan are ready to eat.

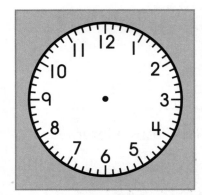

What time is it one half-hour later?

Brainy Book of Time and Money

Drawing the Hour Hand: A Half-Hour Later

Draw the hands on each clock face.

A.   At **8:00**, it starts to rain.

What time is it one half-hour later?

B.   At **11:00**, the sun comes out.

What time is it one half-hour later?

C.   At **3:00**, we skip home from school.

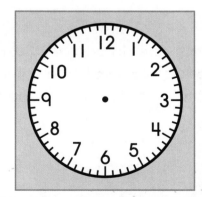

What time is it one half-hour later?

Time Stories

Read each story. Draw the hands on each clock face.

A. Tom makes a HUGE sandwich at
    1:00. He finishes the whole sandwich
    one half-hour later. What time does
    Tom finish the sandwich?

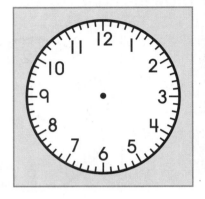

B. Tom gets home from school at **3:00.**
    He goes out to play **30 minutes**
    later. What time does Tom go out to
    play?

C. Tom goes to bed at **8:30**. He falls
    asleep **one half-hour** later. What
    time does Tom fall asleep?

Time Stories

Read each story. Draw the hands on each clock face.

A.   Maria makes lunch at **7:00**. She
     gets on the bus **30 minutes** later.
     What time does she get on the bus?

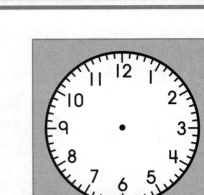

B.   Maria helps make dinner at **5:30**.
     Everyone eats **one half-hour** later.
     What time does everyone eat?

C.   Maria's family plays a game at
     8:30. They stop playing **30 minutes**
     later. What time do they stop playing?

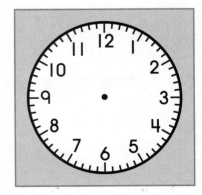

Time Two Ways

Draw the hands on each clock face. Write the time.

A.   At **1:30**, Squirrel hides seven nuts.

B.   At **2:00**, Squirrel runs down the tree to find more nuts.

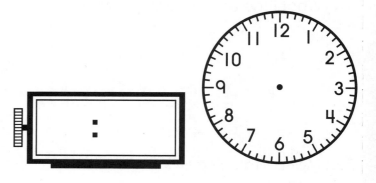

C.   By **3:30**, Squirrel is ready for a long rest.

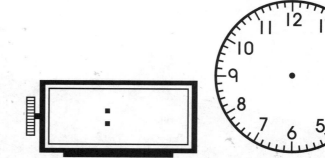

Time Two Ways

Draw the hands on each clock face. Write the time.

A. At **5:30**, Toad hops over to visit Frog.

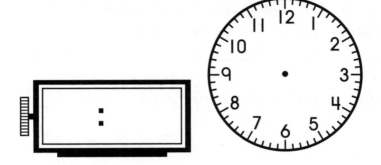

B. At **6:00**, Frog and Toad are sipping
Fine Fly Tea.

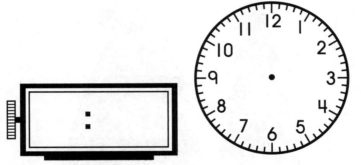

C. At **7:30**, Toad heads home, full of
tea and bug cakes.

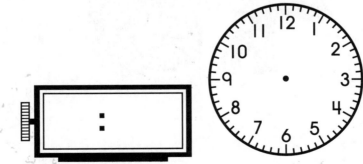

Time Stories

Read the story. Write the time two ways. Choose a time for everyone to eat lunch!

Bear is going on a picnic today with his brother and sister. They leave for
the park at **9:00**. They get to the park at **10:00**. Bear helps carry the food to the picnic
table. Then he gets out his kite. Bear flies his kite at **10:30**. Later,
at _____, everyone has a picnic lunch!

Put the story in order by writing what time Bear did each thing.

A. **Leave for the park**

B. **Get to the park**

C. **Fly kite**

D. **Eat lunch**

Time Stories

Read the story. Write the time two ways. Choose a time for everyone to go home!

Pig wakes up at **7:00**. Pig's grandmother is taking her to the zoo today! They get to the zoo at **10:30**. They walk and walk. They stop to eat at **12:30**. They walk some more. Pig and her grandmother don't get home until _____.
They had a wonderful day!

Put the story in order by writing what time Pig did each thing.

A. _____   B. _____

C. _____   D. _____

Time Puzzles

Read each "time clue." Draw the hands on each clock. Write the time.

A.   It's dark outside.
     Everyone is asleep.

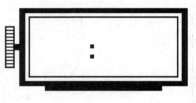

B.   Ring, ring!
     Time to get up.

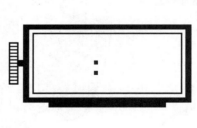

C.   Here comes the school bus.
     Run so you won't
     be late!

D.   I'm hungry! Soon it will
     be time for lunch.

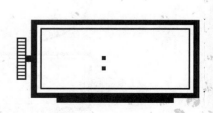

Time Puzzles

Read each "time clue." Draw the hands on each clock. Write the time.

A.   School is out!
    We're going home.

B.   Here comes the mail!
    I hope I get a letter.

C.   It's getting dark.
    Time to go inside.

D.   It's light tonight.
    Look, a big full moon!

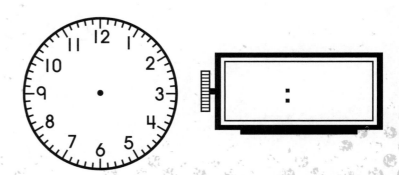

Time to the Quarter-Hour: Introduction

Each **hour** has **60** minutes.
An **hour** has **4 quarter-hours**.
A **quarter-hour** is **15 minutes**.

This clock face shows a quarter of an hour.

From the **12** to the **3** is **15 minutes**.

From the 12 to the 3 is 15 minutes.

_____15_____ minutes after _____8_____ o'clock

is _____8:15_____

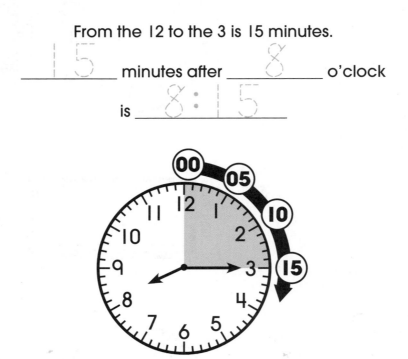

Telling Time

Each **hour** has **4 quarter-hours**. A **quarter-hour** is **15 minutes**.

Write the times.

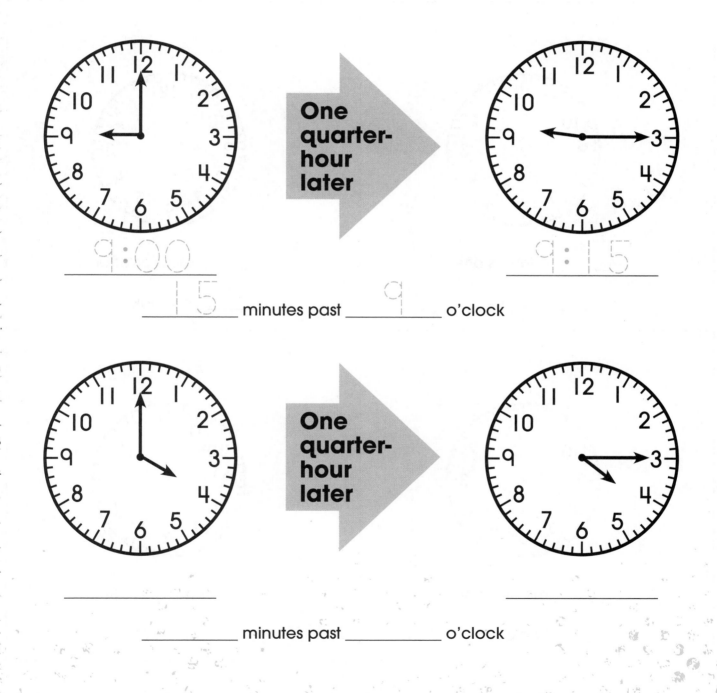

One quarter-hour later

9:00

9:15

_____ minutes past _____ o'clock

One quarter-hour later

_____   _____

_____ minutes past _____ o'clock

Telling Time

Draw the hands. Write the times.

5:15

_____ minutes after

_____ o'clock

10:15

_____ minutes after

_____ o'clock

2:15

_____ minutes after

_____ o'clock

9:15

_____ minutes after

_____ o'clock

Digital Clocks

Your **digital clock** has quarter-hours, too! It also shows **15 minutes**.
Write each quarter-hour.

Digital Clocks

Circle the correct digital time.

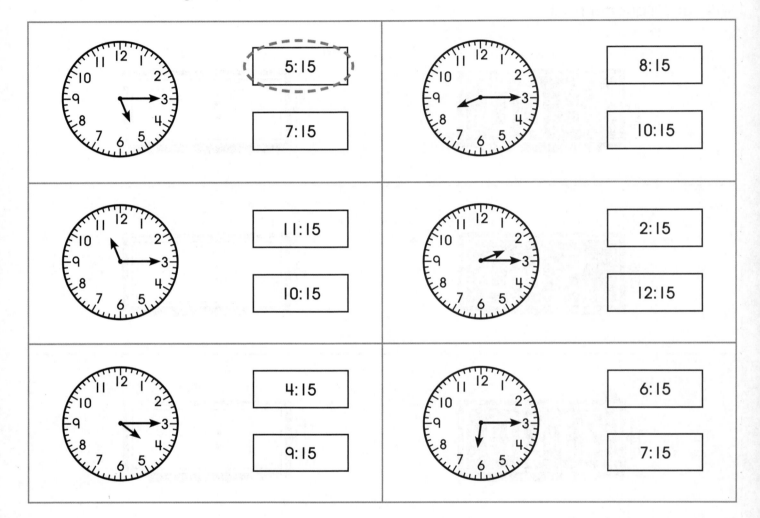

15 minutes past 6 is my dinner time.

Draw the minute hand with an **orange** crayon.

Draw the hour hand with a **purple** crayon.

_____ minutes after _____ o'clock

6:15

Telling Time

Count the numbers by fives to see how many minutes have passed.

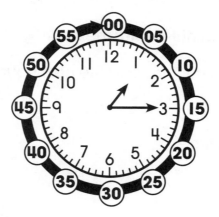

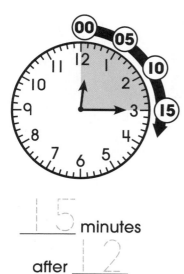

___15___ minutes

after ___12___

___30___ minutes

after ___12___

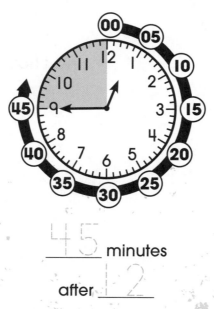

___45___ minutes

after ___12___

Telling Time

Can you speak **"clock time"**?

1. **"Quarter after"** means 15 minutes after the hour.

2. **"Half past"** means 30 minutes after the hour.

3. **"Quarter to"** means 15 minutes until the next hour.

Write the quarter-hours from this time.

_____8_____ o'clock

quarter past _____

half past _____

quarter to _____

next hour: _____ o'clock

Telling Time

Write the time on the digital clocks.

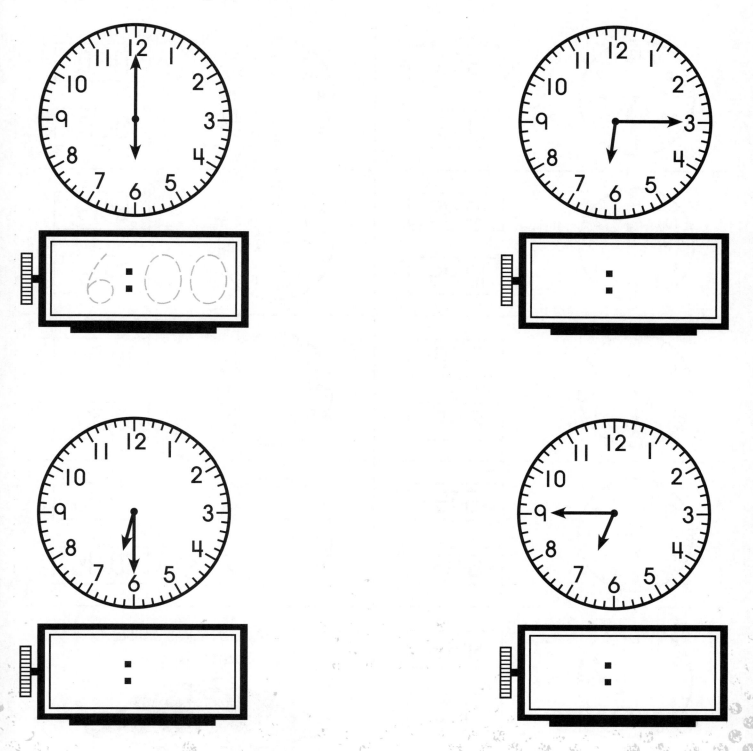

Telling Time

Circle the time.

This pie bakes until a **quarter past 4**.

Time Two Ways

Draw the hands on each clock face. Write the time.

A. Marta **begins** writing a letter **at 3:30**.
She stops **30 minutes later**.

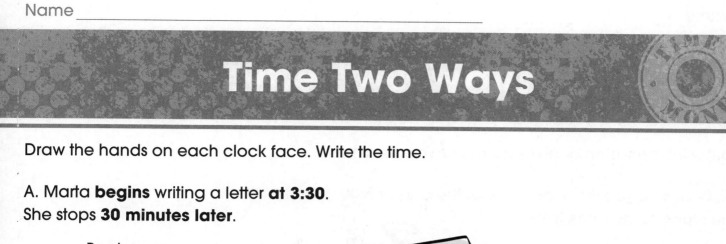

Begins

[:]

Stops

[:]

B. Arnold **begins** playing hockey **at 8:00**.
He **stops 15 minutes later**.

Begins

[:]

Stops

[:]

C. Write your own time story.

_____

_____

_____

Begins

[:]

Stops

[:]

Time Two Ways

Draw the hands on each clock face. Write the time.

A. Darius **begins** throwing balls for the dog at **5:00**.
He **stops 15 minutes later**.

Begins

Stops

| : |

| : |

B. Olga **begins** playing frisbee **at 4:15**.
She **stops 15 minutes later**.

Begins

Stops

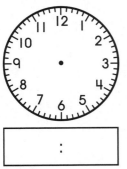

| : |

| : |

C. Write your own time story.

_____

_____

_____

Begins

Stops

| : |

| : |

Time to the Minute: Introduction

Each number on the clock face stands for **5 minutes**.

Count by fives beginning at 12.
Write the numbers here:

__00__ 05 10 15 20 25

It is __25__ minutes after __8__ o'clock.

It is written 8:25.

Count by fives.

__00__ ____ ____ ____ ____ ____ ____

It is _____ minutes after _____ o'clock.

_____:_____

Time to the Minute: Introduction

Write the time both ways.

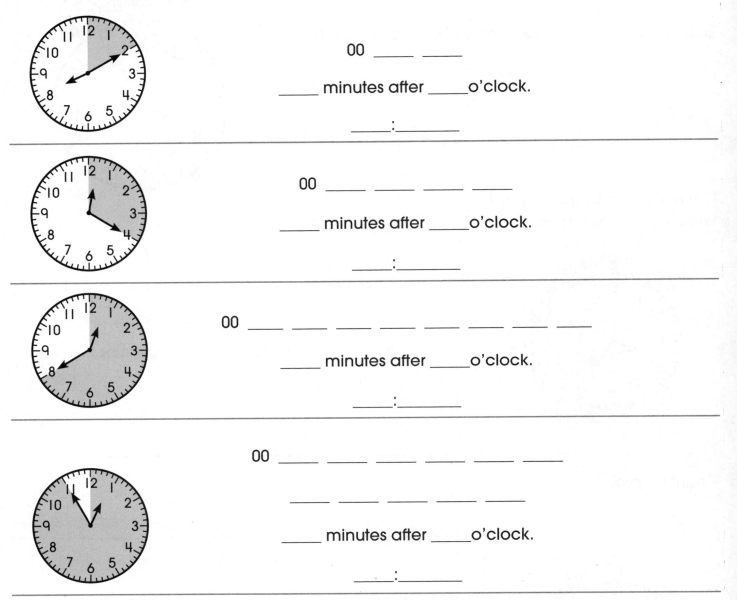

00 _____ _____

_____ minutes after _____ o'clock.

_____:_____

00 _____ _____ _____ _____

_____ minutes after _____ o'clock.

_____:_____

00 _____ _____ _____ _____ _____ _____ _____ _____

_____ minutes after _____ o'clock.

_____:_____

00 _____ _____ _____ _____ _____ _____

_____ _____ _____ _____ _____

_____ minutes after _____ o'clock.

_____:_____

Circle the clocks with times **between 3 o'clock and 9 o'clock**.

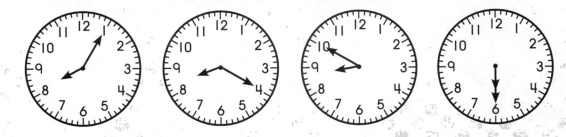

Drawing the Minute Hand

This clock lost its minute hand! Can you help it?

Read the time. Draw the minute hand with a pencil. Color over it with a red crayon.

2:05

__5__ minutes after __2__ o'clock.

Drawing the Minute Hand

Draw and color the minute hand.

12:25

1:20

11:15

3:50

5:30

10:35

Digital Clocks

Can you read a digital clock?
First read the hour.
Then read the minutes.

This clock is read **four twenty**
or **twenty minutes past 4 o'clock**.

Match the digital and analog clocks.

Digital Clocks

Circle the words to match the times.

five twenty  five fifty

six twenty-five  six thirty-five

seven ten  seven twenty

one fifty-five  eleven fifty-five

Writing the Time

Write the times on the worms.

What time is it?

Name _____

Drawing Clock Hands

Draw the hands. Write the time.

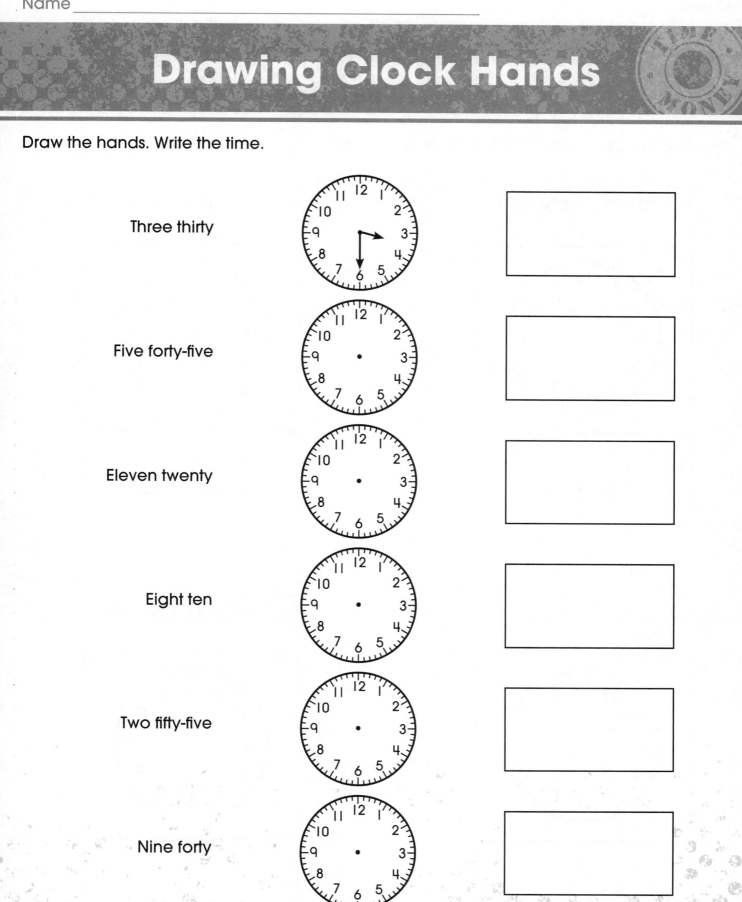

Three thirty

Five forty-five

Eleven twenty

Eight ten

Two fifty-five

Nine forty

Time Two Ways

Draw the hands on each clock face. Write the time.

A.   30 minutes after 6:00

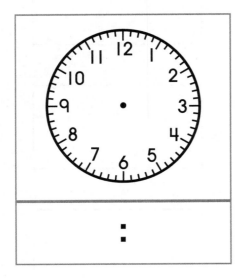

:

B.   20 minutes before 6:00

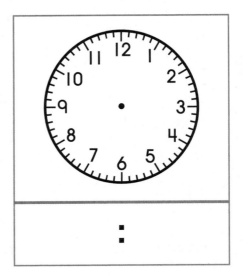

:

C.   Exactly 6 o'clock

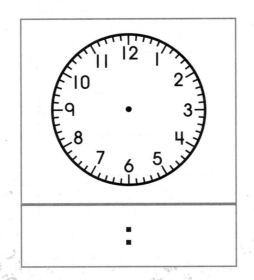

:

D.   20 minutes after 6:00

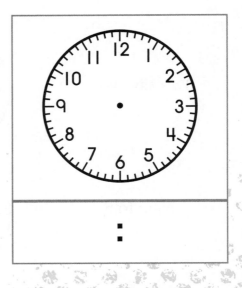

:

Time Two Ways

Draw the hands on each clock face. Write the time.

A. Exactly noon or midnight

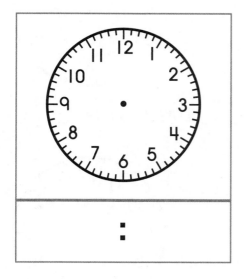

B. Quarter past 12:00

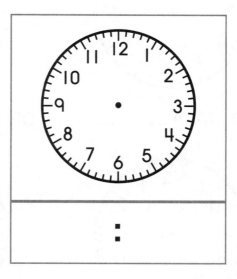

C. 15 minutes before 12:00

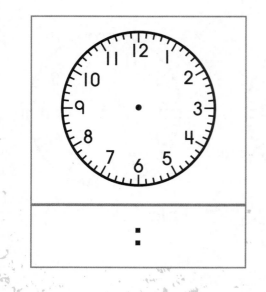

D. Half past 12:00

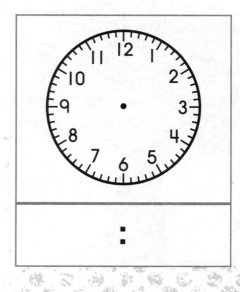

Writing Familiar Times: Family "Time Tree"

Write the time. Draw the hands on each clock.

I get up at _____.

I go to bed at _____.

Lunch is at _____.

Dinner is at _____.

School starts at _____.

School ends at _____.

Recess is at _____.

I play at _____.

Time Lapse: Minutes

How much time did each activity take?

1. Jimmy played darts from 1:20 till 1:40.

   He played for __20__ minutes.

2. Marietta rode a pony for 15 minutes.

   She began at 1:00.

   She finished at _____ : _____

3. She had so much fun, she rode another 15 minutes.

   She finished at _____ : _____

Time Lapse: Minutes

How much time did each activity take?

1. Tim worked at the snow cone booth. The first clock shows the time he started. He worked 1 hour and 30 minutes. Show the time he finished on the second clock.

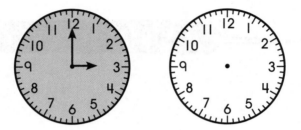

2. Andrea won the juggling contest. She kept the balls in the air for 5 minutes. She began juggling at 1:25. She finished at _____ : _____.

   Circle the clock which shows the correct time.

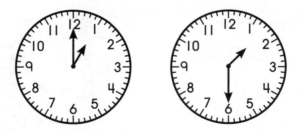

Write the time.

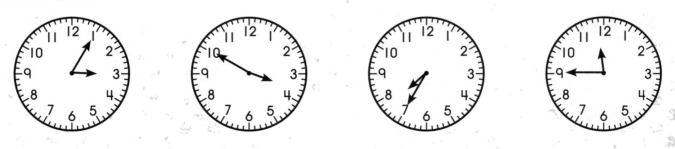

_____   _____   _____   _____

Drawing Clock Hands

Read each story. Draw the hands on each clock face.

A.   Frog sees a fly at 1:00.
     He catches the fly and eats it 60 minutes later.

Sees fly   **Eats fly**

B.   Frog hops out of the water at 2:00.
     Frog hops back in the water 40 minutes later.

Hops out   **Hops back in**

   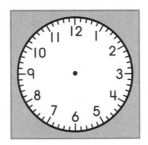

C.   Frog sits on a lily pad at 3:00.
     He swims away 45 minutes later.

Sits on lily pad   **Swims away**

Drawing Clock Hands

Read each story. Draw the hands on each clock face.

A.   Rabbit hops into his garden at 6:00. He finishes working in the garden one and one-half hours later.

Hops in garden

Finishes work

B.   Rabbit gets out lettuce and carrots at 8:30. He finishes eating 45 minutes later.

Gets out lettuce and carrots

Finishes eating

C.   Rabbit lies down for a nap at 4:00. He wakes up and hip-hops away 55 minutes later.

Lies down

Wakes up

Time Stories

Read the story. Write the times on each digital clock.

Val and Phil Camp Out

Val and Phil go out to the backyard at 6:00. They put up their tent. This takes them 1 hour and 30 minutes. They get in the tent and talk for 1 hour. Then they fall asleep. They sleep for 2 hours, until a dog barks and wakes them up.

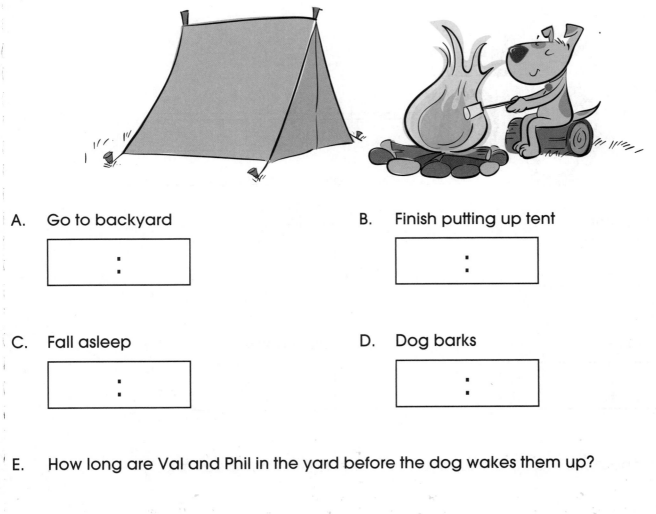

A. Go to backyard

| : |

B. Finish putting up tent

| : |

C. Fall asleep

| : |

D. Dog barks

| : |

E. How long are Val and Phil in the yard before the dog wakes them up?

_____ hours and _____ minutes

Name _____

Time Stories

Read the story. Write the times on each digital clock.

Mike and Maria Go Skating

Mike and Maria leave home at 3:30. They ride their bikes to the ice-skating rink. This takes one half-hour. They skate and leave the rink 2 hours later. They get on their bikes and arrive home 40 minutes after leaving the rink.

A.   Leave home

```
  [   :   ]
```

B.   Get to rink

```
  [   :   ]
```

C.   Leave rink

```
  [   :   ]
```

D.   Arrive home

```
  [   :   ]
```

E.   How long does Mike & Maria's trip to the skating rink and back take?

_____ hours and _____ minutes

Time Stories

Read each time story. Write the time on each clock.

Benito went for a ride on the roller coaster. He got on the roller coaster at 2:30. He rode for 15 minutes. What time did he get off?

A. **Start ride**
    [:]

B. **Get off**
    [:]

Valerie and her sister went hiking. They started hiking at 9:00. They hiked for one hour and 30 minutes. What time did they stop hiking?

C. **Start hike**
    [:]

D. **Finish hike**
    [:]

Ben and his mother rode the subway for 20 minutes. They got off the subway at 4:30. When did Ben and his mother get on the subway?

E. **Get on**
    [:]

F. **Get off**
    [:]

Time Stories

Read each time story. Write the time on each clock.

Andrea and her sister walked by the lake. They started walking at 2:15. They walked for one hour and 15 minutes. What time did they stop walking?

A. **Start walking**

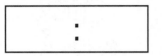

B. **Stop walking**

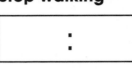

Berta gave her dog Maria a bath. She started washing at 7:40. Maria hates baths. It took Berta 50 minutes to wash the dog. They both got wet! When did she finish?

C. **Start bath**

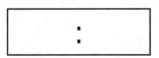

D. **Finish bath**

Sergei played frisbee with his brother for 40 minutes. They stopped playing at 7:30. When did Sergei start playing frisbee?

E. **Start playing**

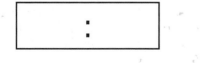

F. **Stop playing**

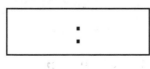

Name _____

Time Puzzles

Write any time that fits the time clues.

A.   Between 11:00 and 12:00

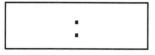

B.   Between 30 minutes after 2:00 and 3:00

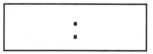

C.   After quarter-past 7:00 and before 8:00

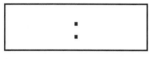

D.   Make up your own time clues.
     Ask a friend to solve your time puzzle!

_____

_____

_____

_____

Time Puzzles

Write any time that fits the time clues.

A. Between 4:15 and 5:15

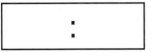

B. After 6:00 and before quarter to 7:00

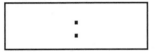

C. Between noon and 1:00

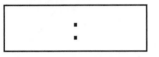

D. Make up your own time clues.
    Ask a friend to solve your time puzzle!

_____

_____

_____

_____

Time Stories

Read the story. Write the time on each clock.

Erin and her brother Harry were shopping for dinner. First they went into the bakery at 5:00 to buy fresh bread. This took 5 minutes. Next they walked to the market for vegetables and cereal. This took them 20 minutes. Then they walked next door for a treat at Fanny's Famous Fudge. This took them 15 minutes. Then they met their brother Andrew outside.

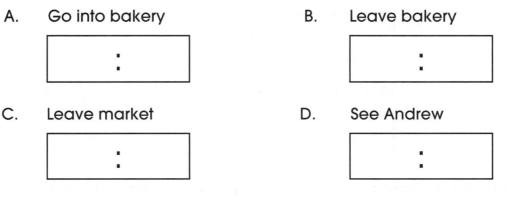

A.   Go into bakery

B.   Leave bakery

C.   Leave market

D.   See Andrew

E.   **How long** had Erin and Harry been shopping when they saw Andrew?

_____

F.   Make up your own story about shopping. What do you do, and how long does each thing take? Make up a starting time. Use your clock to find the ending time.

Time Stories

Read the story. Write the time on each clock.

Hanna and Shawn got to the fair at 3:00. They threw balls at the clown's pocket for 10 minutes. No luck! Then they rode the Big Dipper for 30 minutes. They got wet! After this they ate pizza for 15 minutes. Then they saw their friend Monique.

A. Go in fair

B. Stop throwing balls

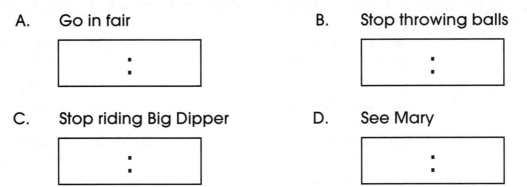

C. Stop riding Big Dipper

D. See Mary

E. **How long** had Hanna and Shawn been at the fair when they saw Monique?

_____

F. Make up your own story about being at a fair. What do you do, and how long does each thing take? Make up a starting time. Use your clock to find the ending time.

Telling Time: Using Charts

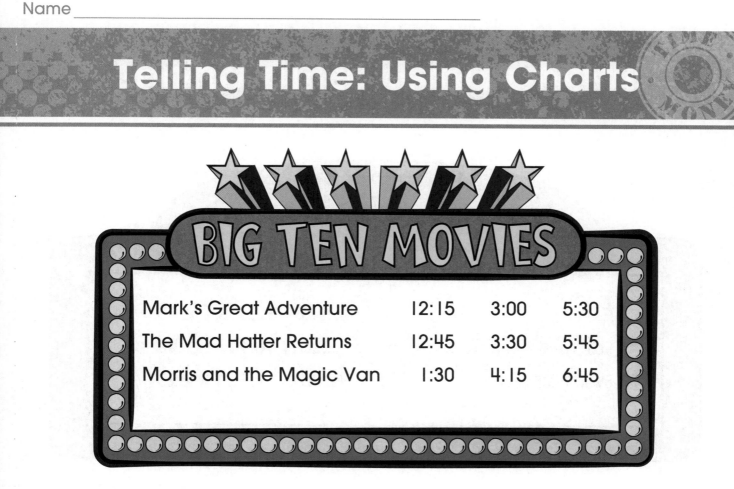

Use the chart. Write the time that each pair went to a movie.

A.   Barry and his brother went to the movie that began closest to 4:00.

Movie: _____

Began at: _____

B.   Andrea and her friend went to the movie that began closest to 1:00.

Movie: _____

Began at: _____

C.   **Make up** your own time puzzle about these movie times.

Telling Time: Using Charts

MAIN AIRPORT

MONDAY DEPARTURES:

Gull Air	10:45	12:10	1:45
Far West Airlines	9:25	10:10	11:40
Swift Flights	12:30	1:15	2:20

Use the chart. Write the time that each pair took a flight.

A. Teresa and her aunt flew on the plane that left closest
to 10:30.
Airline: _____
Left at: _____

B. Leticia and her father flew on the plane that left closest
to 12:30.
Airline: _____
Left at: _____

C. **Make up** your own time puzzle about the airport.

Name _____

This is a **penny**.

It is worth **1 cent**.
It has **2 sides**.

front   back

This is the **cent symbol**.
Trace it.

⊄

Color the pennies brown.

Pennies: Introduction

Find each penny. Color it brown.

How many pennies did you find? _____

Count the pennies.

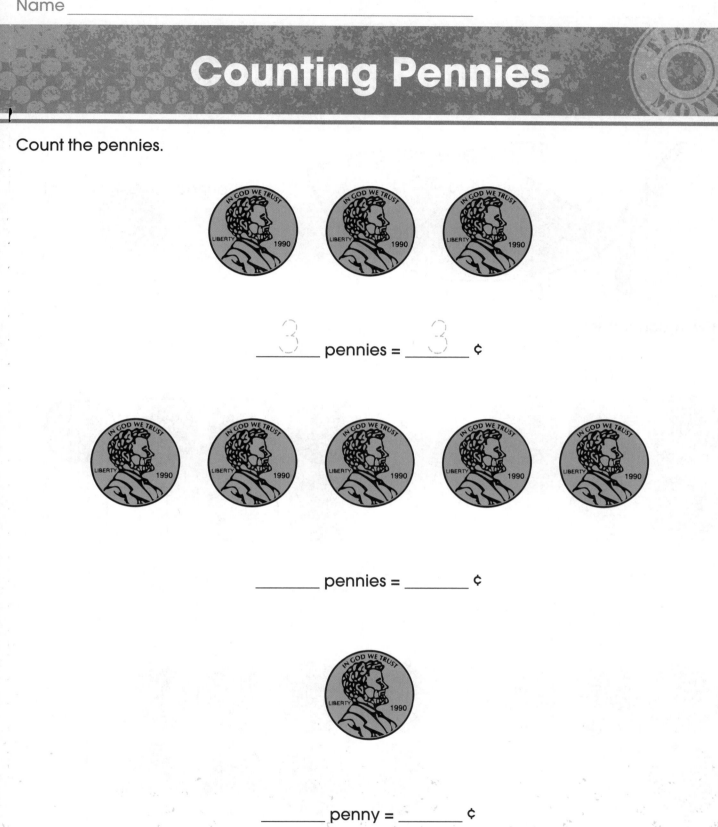

_____ pennies = _____ ¢

_____ pennies = _____ ¢

_____ penny = _____ ¢

Counting Pennies

I penny    I cent

How much money?

Example:

= 5 ¢

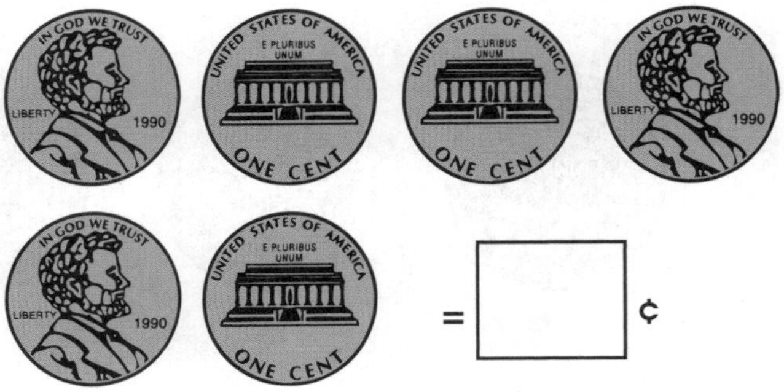

= [ ] ¢

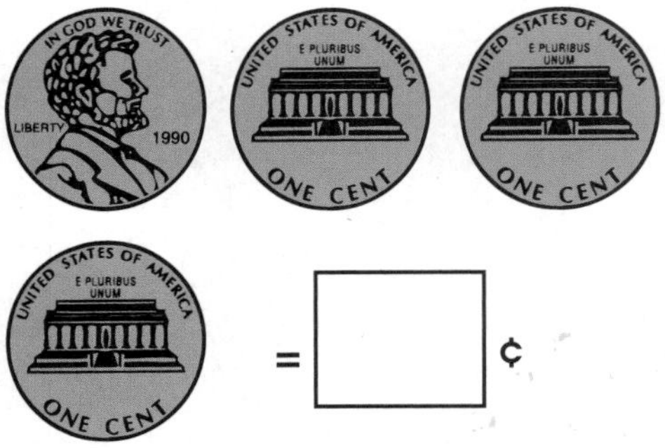

= [ ] ¢

= [ ] ¢

Counting Pennies

Count the pennies. How many cents?

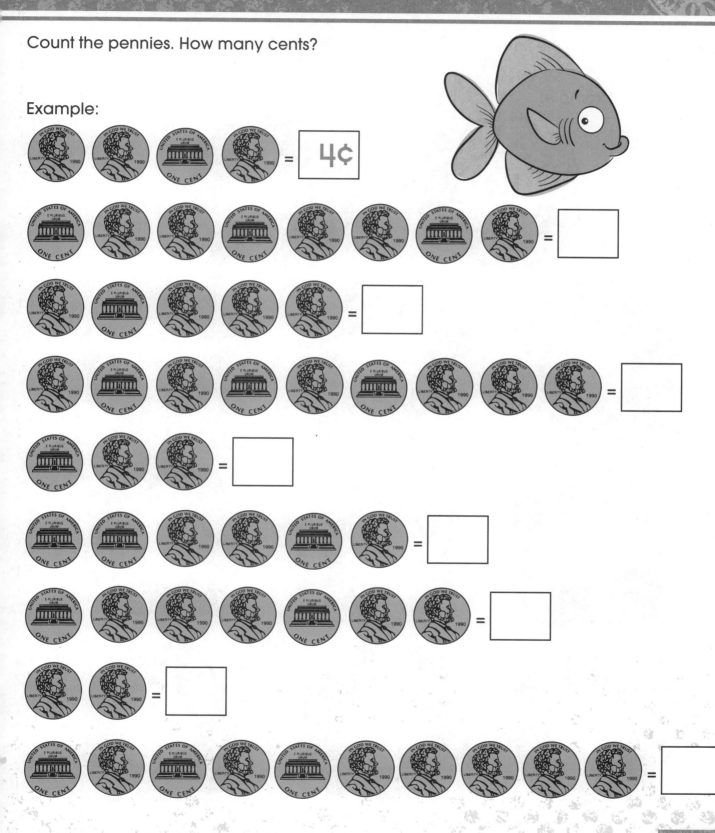

Example:

= 4¢

Counting Pennies

Count the pennies on the flowers. Write the cents in the center.

Example:

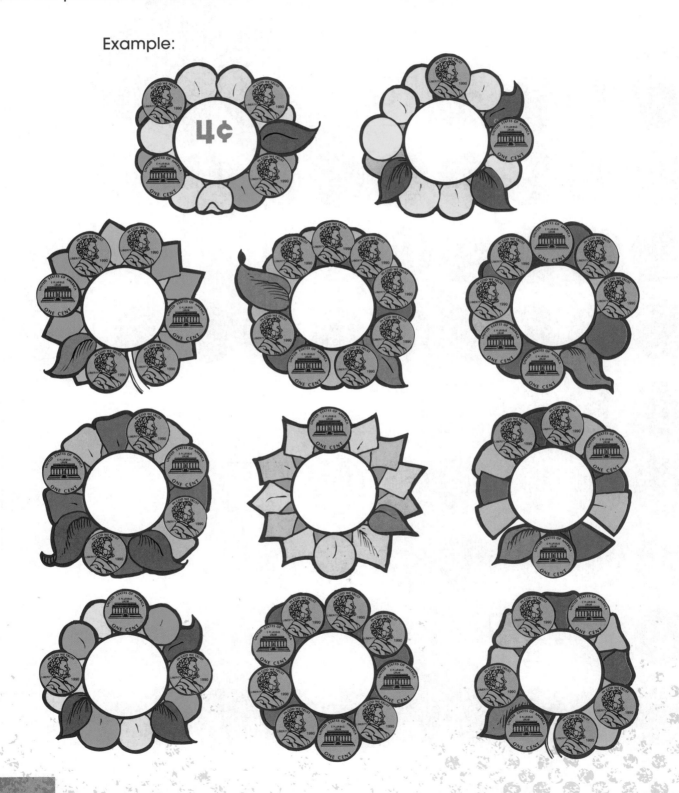

Counting Pennies

Draw a line from the pennies to the right numbers.

Example:

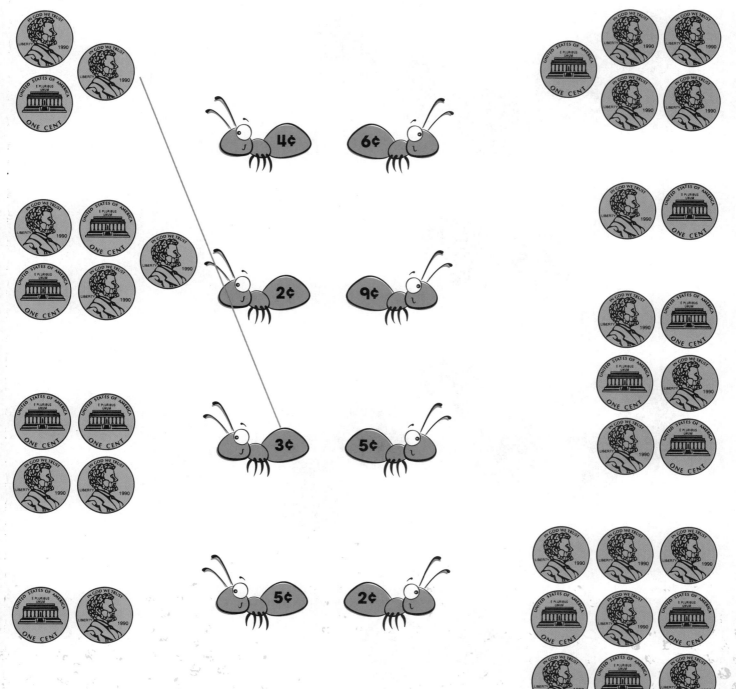

Counting Pennies

Count the pennies in each chain. Draw a line to the number of pennies.

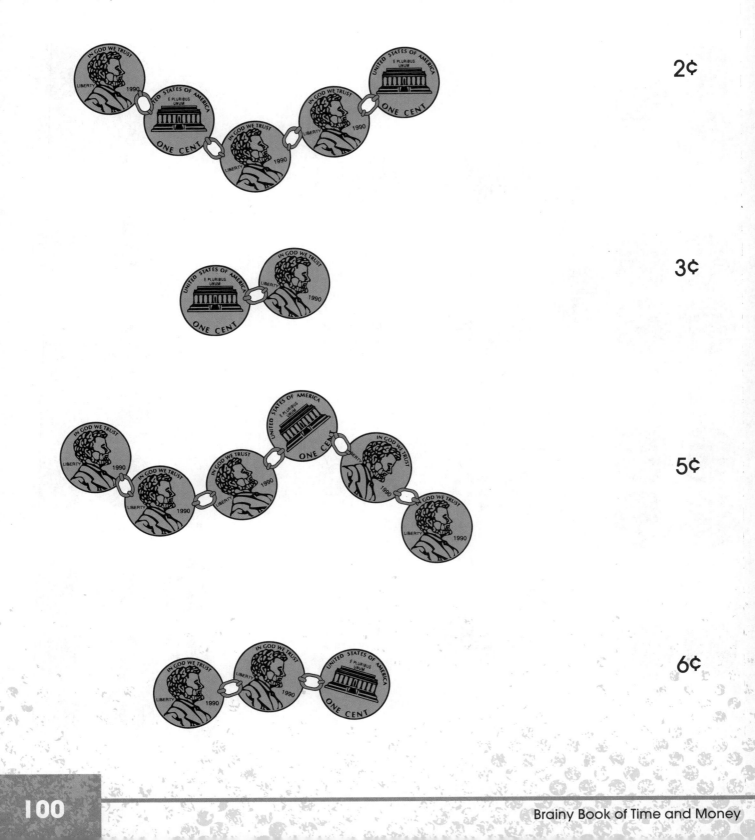

2¢

3¢

5¢

6¢

Counting Pennies

Count the pennies in each group. Match each group to the correct bag.

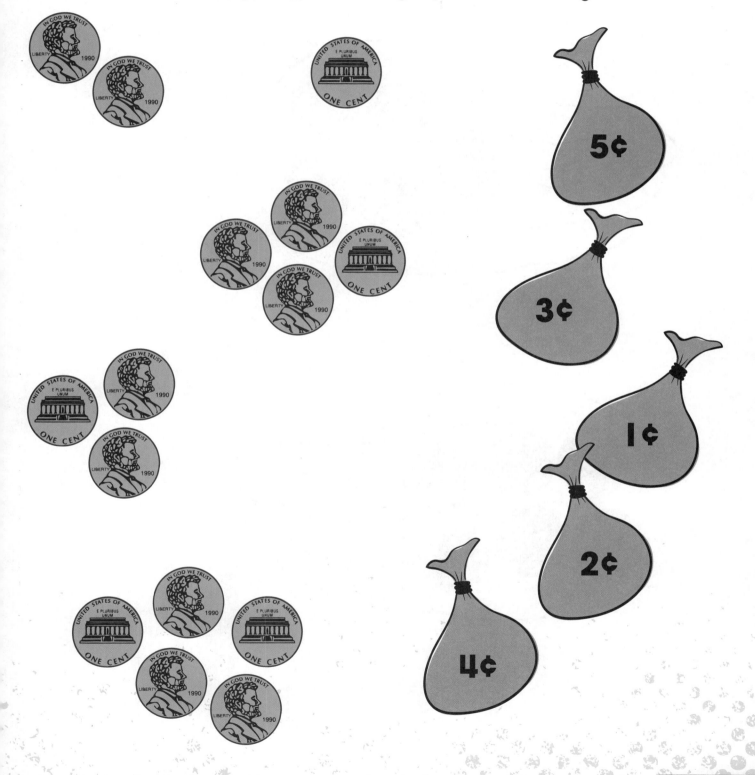

Counting Pennies

Count the money. How much?

A.

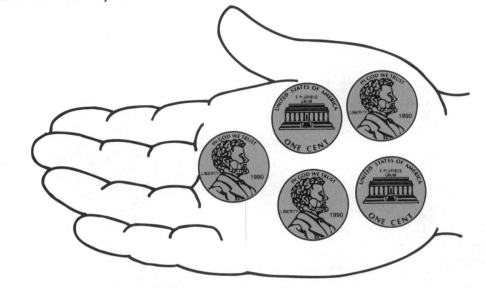

_____ ¢

B.

_____ ¢

Counting Pennies

Count the money. Write the amount.

A.

_____ ¢

B.

_____ ¢

C. Who has more money?
Circle the answer.

Nickels: Introduction

Color the nickels silver.

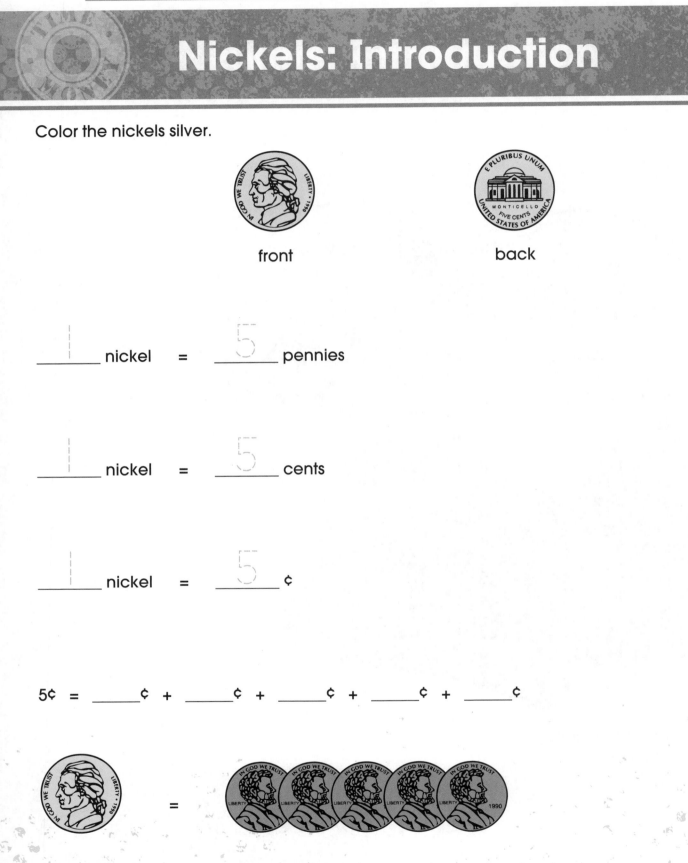

front   back

_____ nickel = _____ pennies

_____ nickel = _____ cents

_____ nickel = _____ ¢

5¢ = _____¢ + _____¢ + _____¢ + _____¢ + _____¢

=

Here is a **penny**. Color it brown.

And here is a **nickel**. Color it silver.

I penny = _____ cent

I penny = _____ ¢

I nickel = _____ cents

I nickel = _____ ¢

Make a cent symbol here: _____

Counting with Nickels and Pennies

Count this money. Begin by saying "5" for the nickel and add 1 for each penny.

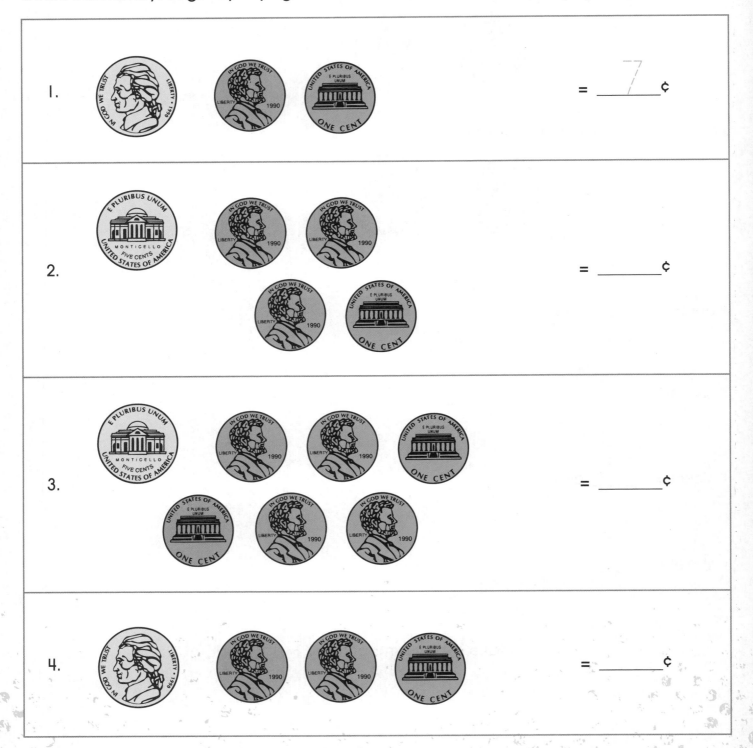

1. = ___7___ ¢

2. = _____ ¢

3. = _____ ¢

4. = _____ ¢

Brainy Book of Time and Money

Count the money. Start with the nickel. Then count the pennies. Write the amount.

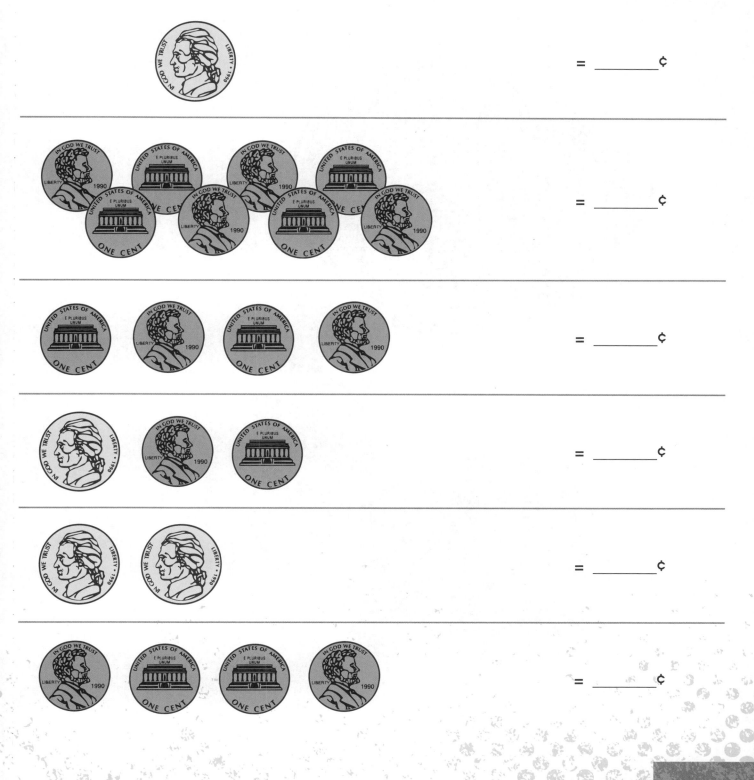

= _____ ¢

= _____ ¢

= _____ ¢

= _____ ¢

= _____ ¢

= _____ ¢

Counting with Nickels and Pennies

Count the money. Start with the nickel. Then count the pennies. Write the amount of money.

A.

_____ ¢

B.

_____ ¢

Name _____

Count the money. Write the amount.

A.

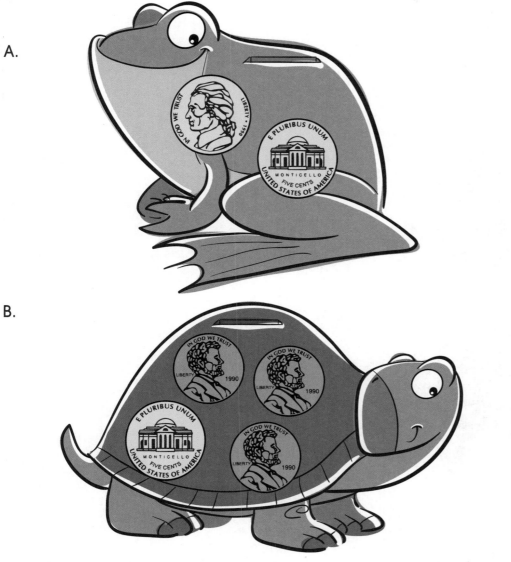

_____ ¢

B.

_____ ¢

C. Who has more money?
Circle the answer.

Counting with Nickels and Pennies

Each **nickel** is worth **5 cents**. Write how much these nickels are worth.

 = _____¢

 = _____¢

= _____¢   =   _____¢

 = _____¢

= _____¢

= _____¢   =   _____¢

 = _____¢

= _____¢

= _____¢

= _____¢   =   _____¢

Nickels: Counting by Fives

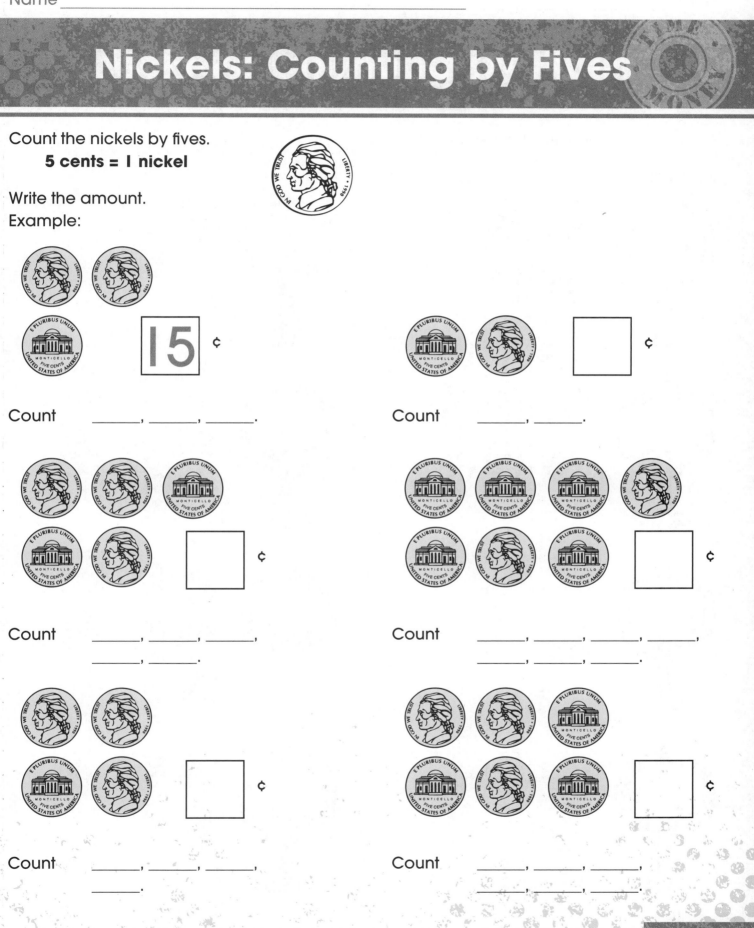

Count the nickels by fives.

5 cents = 1 nickel

Write the amount.
Example:

⬜ 15 ¢

Count _____, _____, _____.

⬜ ¢

Count _____, _____.

⬜ ¢

Count _____, _____, _____,
_____, _____.

⬜ ¢

Count _____, _____, _____, _____,
_____, _____, _____.

⬜ ¢

Count _____, _____, _____,
_____.

⬜ ¢

Count _____, _____, _____,
_____, _____, _____.

Nickels: Counting by Fives

Count the nickels. Write the money in the meter.

Example:

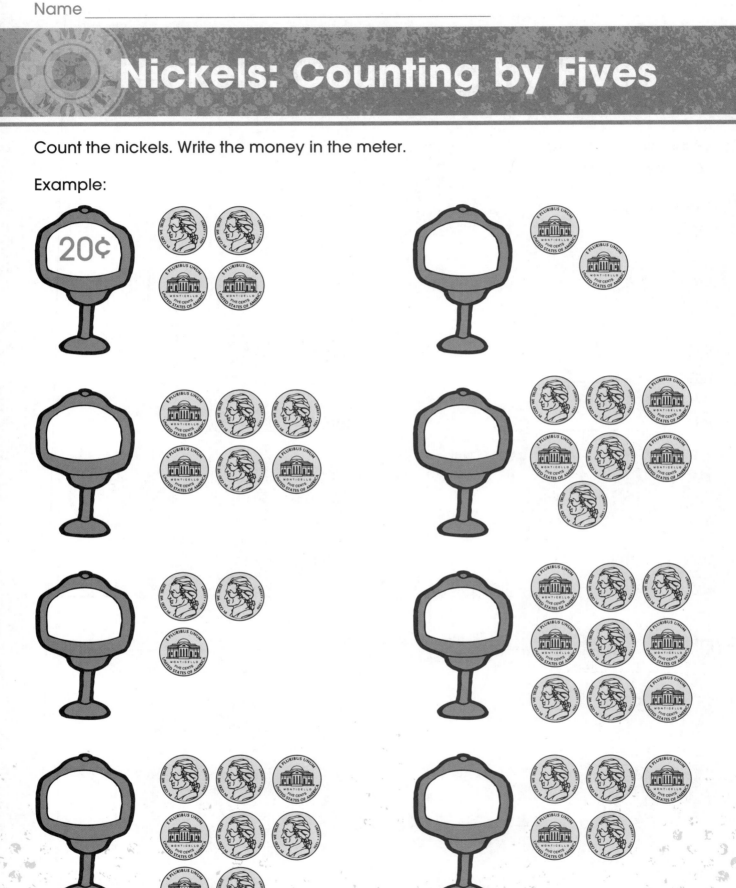

Name_____

How much money is in each hive?

Example:

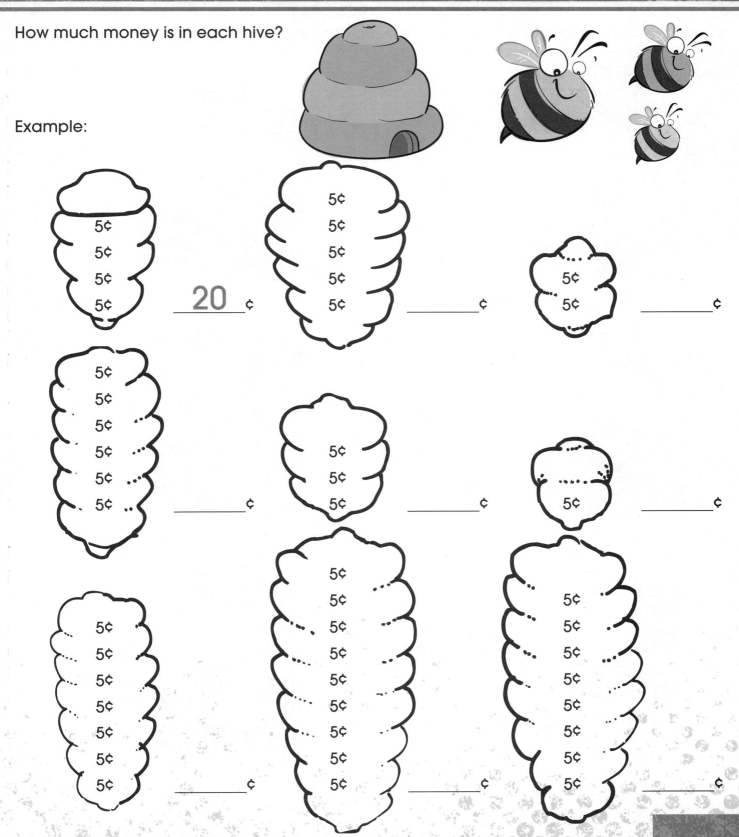

Count the coins. Write the amount next to each bunny.

Example:

_____7____ ¢

_____ ¢

_____ ¢

_____ ¢

_____ ¢

_____ ¢

Counting with Nickels and Pennies

Count the coins. Draw a line to match each owl with the same amount of money.

Example:

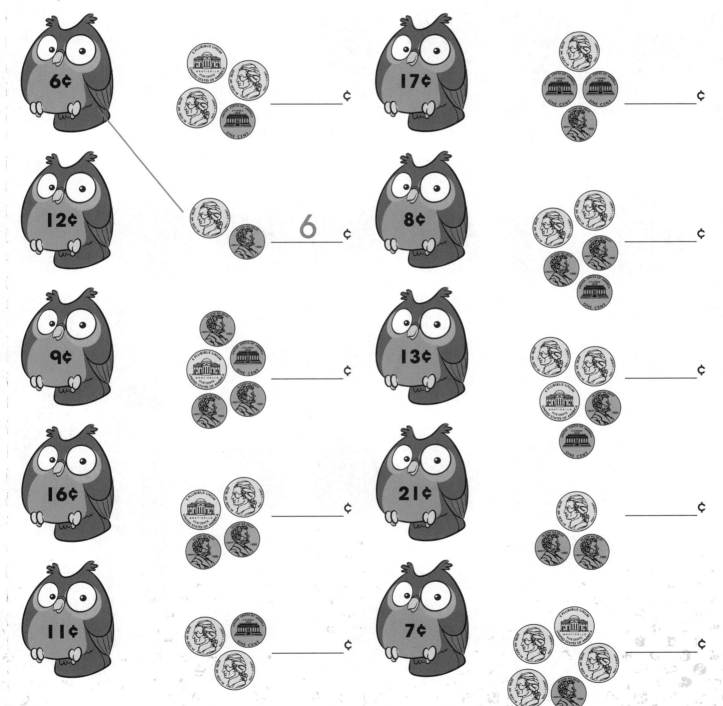

Counting with Nickels and Pennies

Count the money. Start with nickels. Then count the pennies.

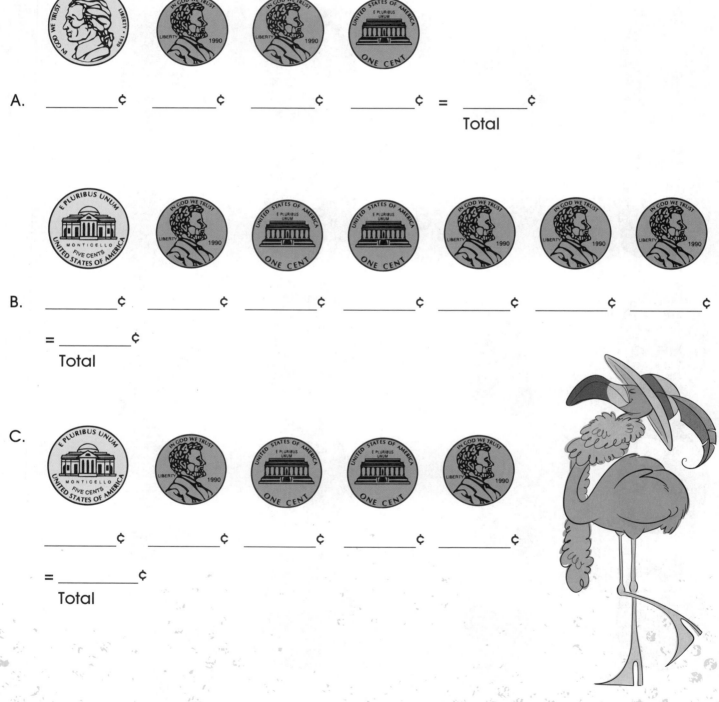

A. _____ ¢   _____ ¢   _____ ¢   _____ ¢ = _____ ¢
                                                              Total

B. _____ ¢   _____ ¢   _____ ¢   _____ ¢   _____ ¢   _____ ¢   _____ ¢

= _____ ¢
   Total

C. _____ ¢   _____ ¢   _____ ¢   _____ ¢   _____ ¢

= _____ ¢
   Total

Counting with Nickels and Pennies

Look at the price on each toy. Color it if there are enough nickels.

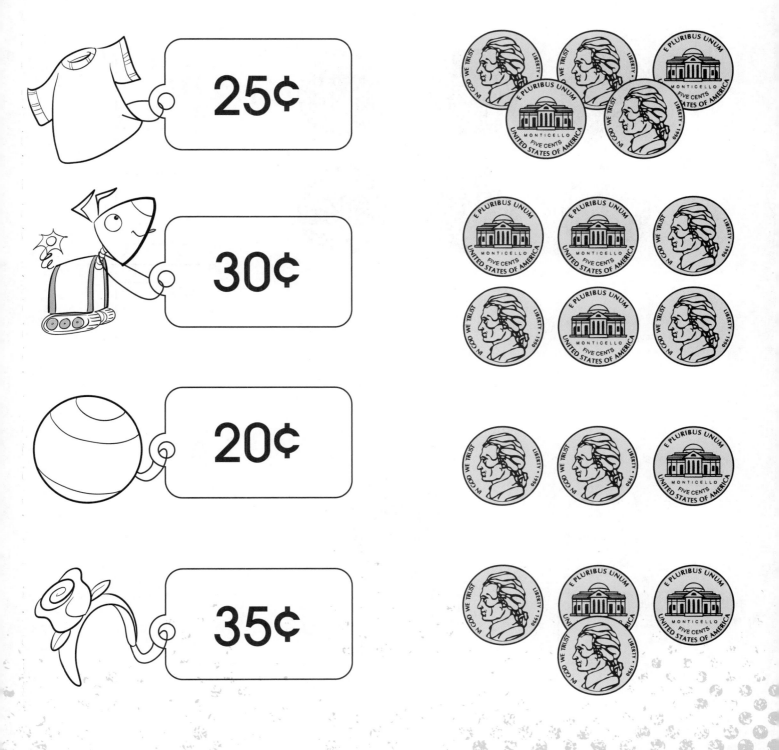

Adding with Nickels and Pennies

Adding money is fun and easy! Write how much money there is in all.

$$\square \ ¢$$
$$+ \ \square \ ¢$$
$$\overline{}$$
$$\square \ ¢ \ \text{in all}$$

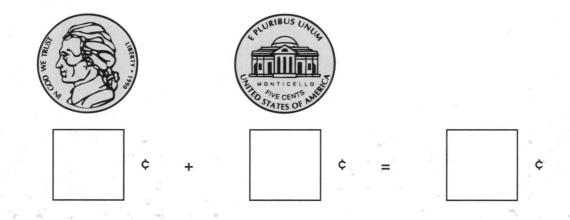

$$\square \ ¢ \ + \ \square \ ¢ \ = \ \square \ ¢$$

Adding with Nickels and Pennies

☐ ¢

+ ☐ ¢
_____

☐ ¢

Draw groups of pennies and nickels here. Write an addition sentence using the coins you drew. Color the coins.

Adding with Nickels and Pennies

Write an addition sentence for each problem.

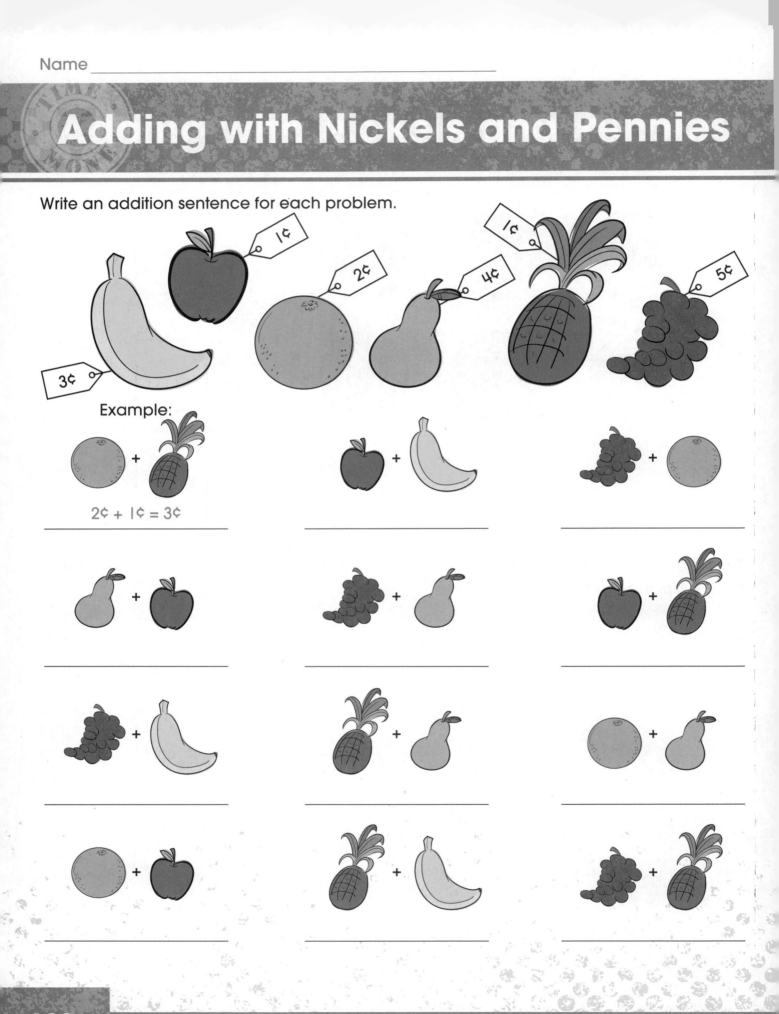

Example:

2¢ + 1¢ = 3¢

Kristen is having a birthday party. Let's see what she bought for her 3 friends.

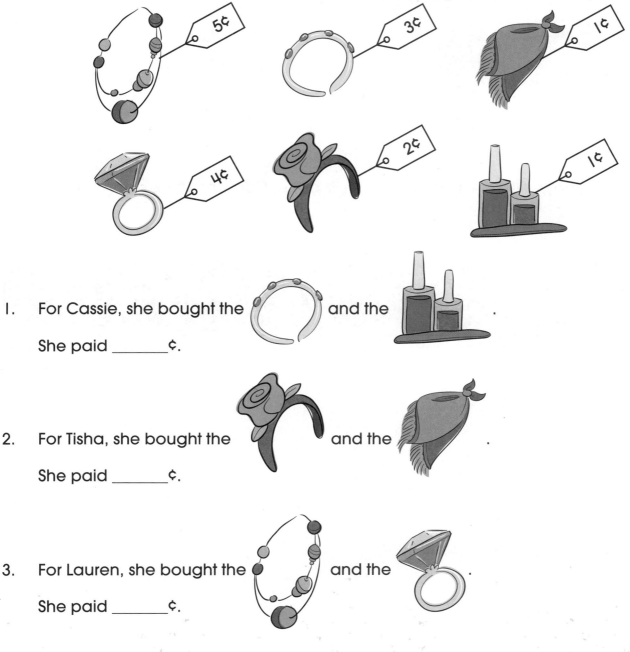

1. For Cassie, she bought the ⬭ and the 💅 .

    She paid _____¢.

2. For Tisha, she bought the 🎀 and the 🧣 .

    She paid _____¢.

3. For Lauren, she bought the 📿 and the 💍 .

    She paid _____¢.

Dimes: Introduction

A dime can buy more than a penny or a nickel.

front

back

Each side of a dime is different. It has ridges on its edge. Color the dime silver.

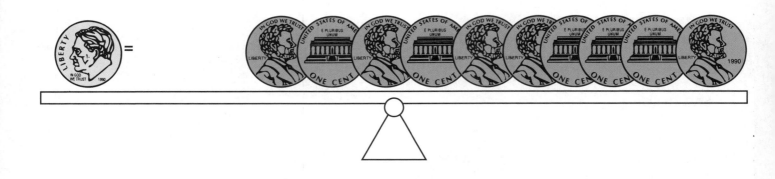

_____ dime = _____ pennies

_____ dime = _____ cents

_____ dime = _____ ¢

Counting with Dimes and Pennies

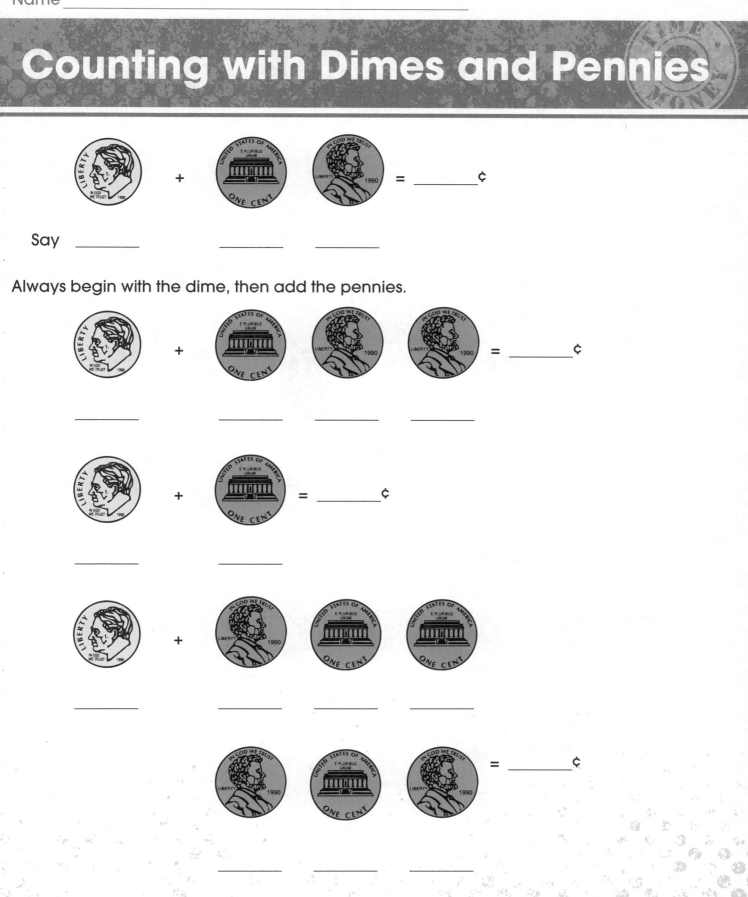

Say _____   _____   _____

Always begin with the dime, then add the pennies.

_____   _____   _____   _____

_____   _____

_____

_____   _____   _____

_____   _____   _____

Counting with Dimes and Pennies

Count the money. Write the amount.

A.

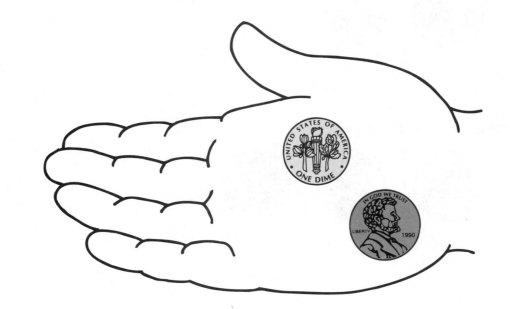

_____ ¢

B.

_____ ¢

Name _____

Count by tens. Write the number. Circle the group with more.

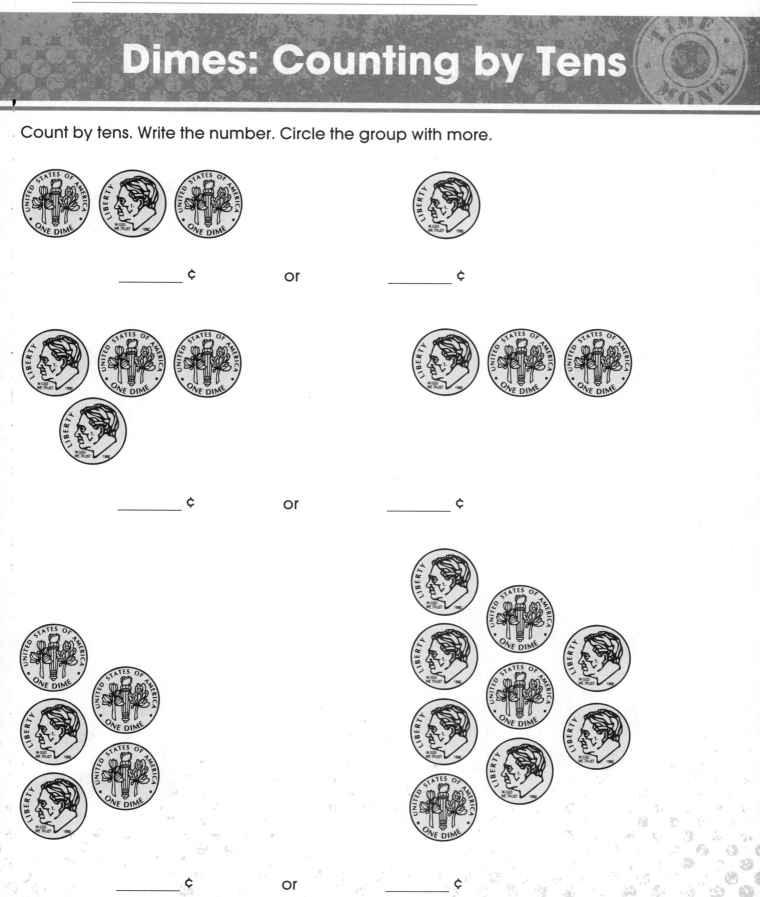

_____¢   or   _____¢

_____¢   or   _____¢

_____¢   or   _____¢

Counting with Dimes and Pennies

Count the dimes by tens. Then count the pennies. How much?

Example:

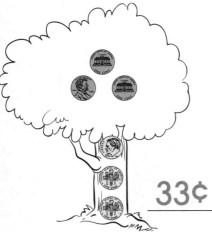 33¢

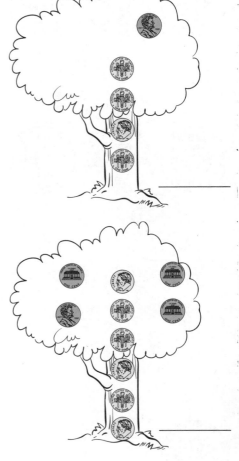

Look carefully at these dimes and nickels. Circle two nickels, then two more, until all the nickels are circled.

Then count by tens to see how much money is here.

I see _____ ¢

Counting with Dimes and Nickels

Count the money. Start with dimes, then count the nickels. Write the amount.

A.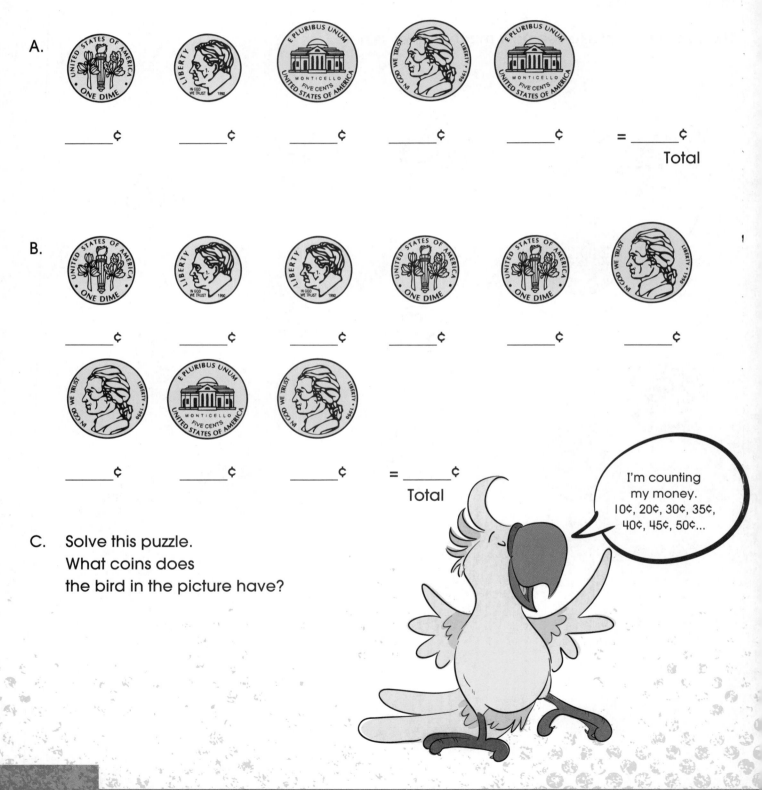

_____¢   _____¢   _____¢   _____¢   _____¢   = _____¢
                                                              Total

B.

_____¢   _____¢   _____¢   _____¢   _____¢   _____¢

_____¢   _____¢   _____¢   = _____¢
                                      Total

C. Solve this puzzle.
    What coins does
    the bird in the picture have?

I'm counting
my money.
10¢, 20¢, 30¢, 35¢,
40¢, 45¢, 50¢...

Counting with Dimes, Nickels, and Pennies

Count the money. Start with the dime. Write the amount.

A.

_____ ¢

B.

_____ ¢

C. Who has more money?
Circle the answer.

Counting with Dimes, Nickels, and Pennies

Count the money. Start with the dime. Write the amount.

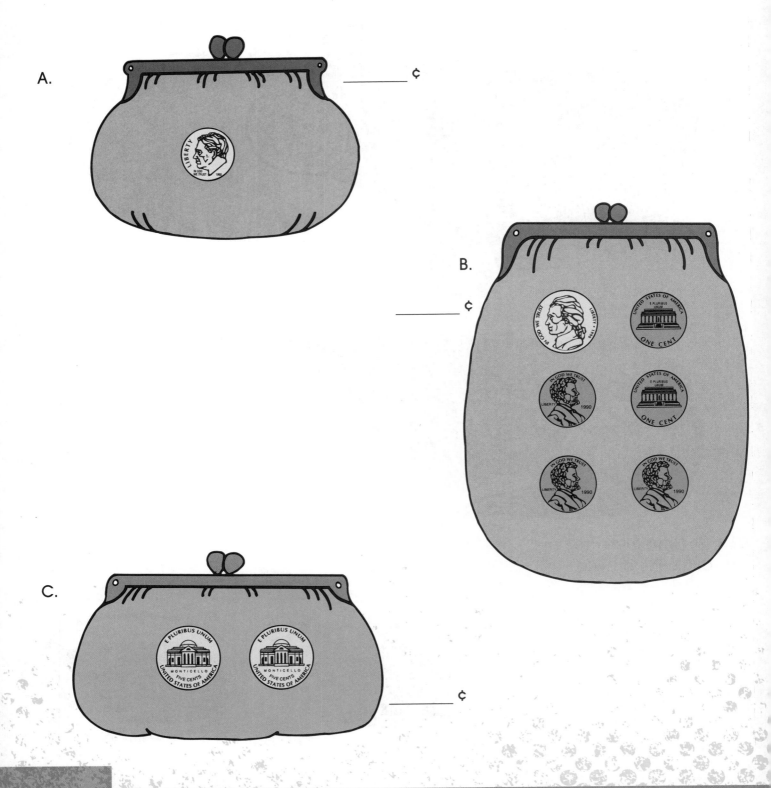

A. _____ ¢

B. _____ ¢

C. _____ ¢

Count the money. Start with the dime. Write the amount.

A.

_____ ¢

B.

_____ ¢

Counting with Dimes, Nickels, and Pennies

Count the money. Start with the dime. Write the amount.

A.

_____ ¢

B.

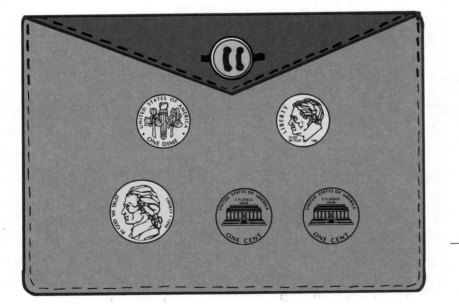

_____ ¢

Counting with Dimes, Nickels, and Pennies

Count the money on each belt. Write the amount under the belt.

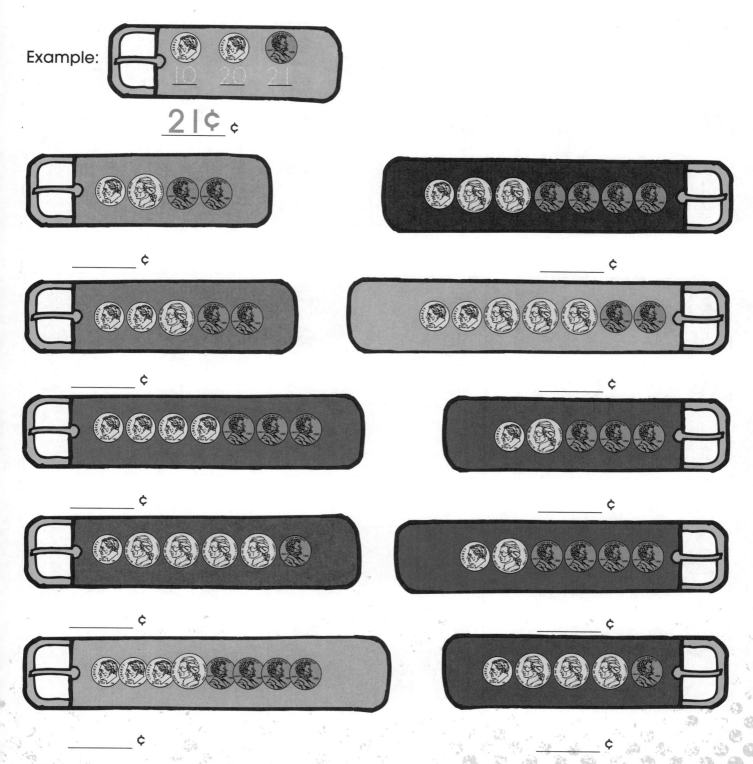

Example:

10   20   21

__21__¢ ¢

_____ ¢

_____ ¢

_____ ¢

_____ ¢

_____ ¢

_____ ¢

_____ ¢

_____ ¢

_____ ¢

_____ ¢

Counting with Dimes, Nickels, and Pennies

Count the coins. Circle the set with more money.

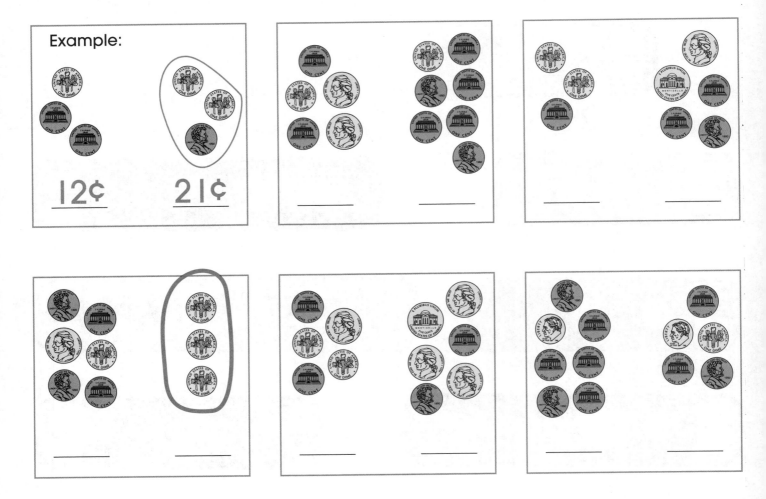

Example:

12¢   21¢

_____ _____

_____ _____

_____ _____

_____ _____

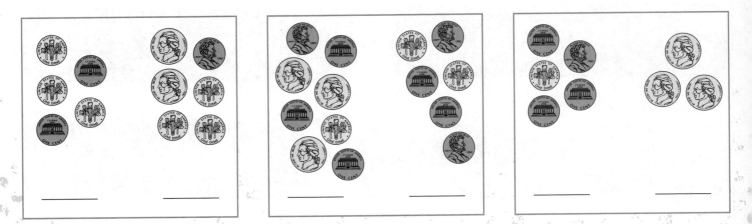

_____ _____

_____ _____

_____ _____

Brainy Book of Time and Money

Counting with Dimes, Nickels, and Pennies

Circle the coins to equal the right amount.

Example:

Counting with Dimes, Nickels, and Pennies

Circle the coins to show the right amount.

Example:

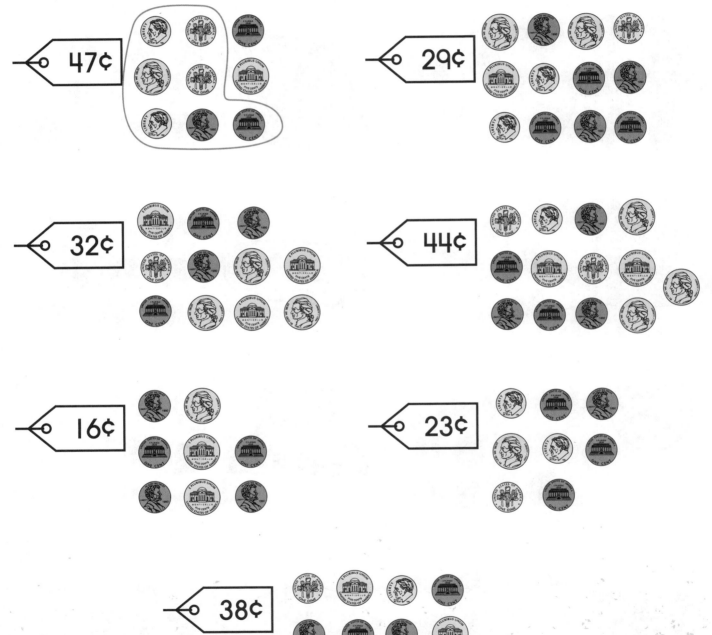

Counting with Dimes, Nickels, and Pennies

Draw a line from the coins to the right amount.

Example:

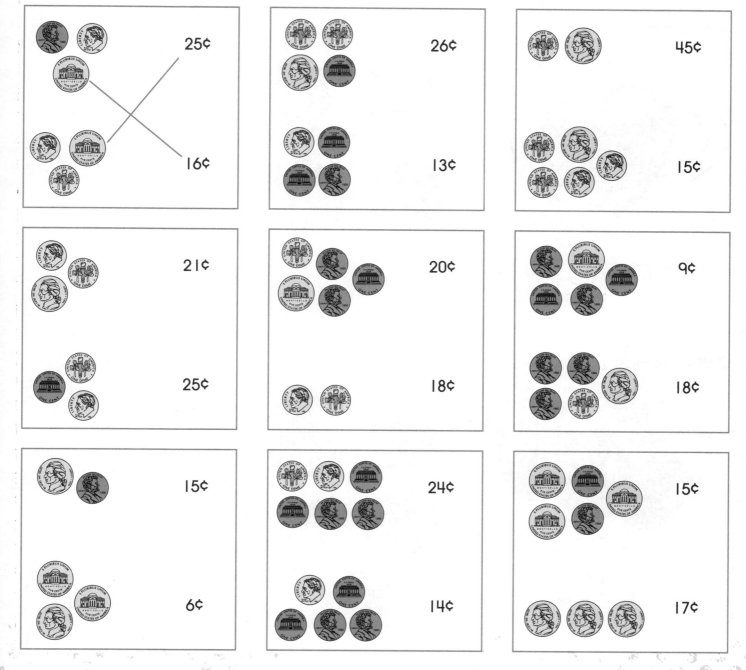

Subtracting with Dimes, Nickels, and Pennies

"X" the coins needed. Write how much money is left.

José wants

He has

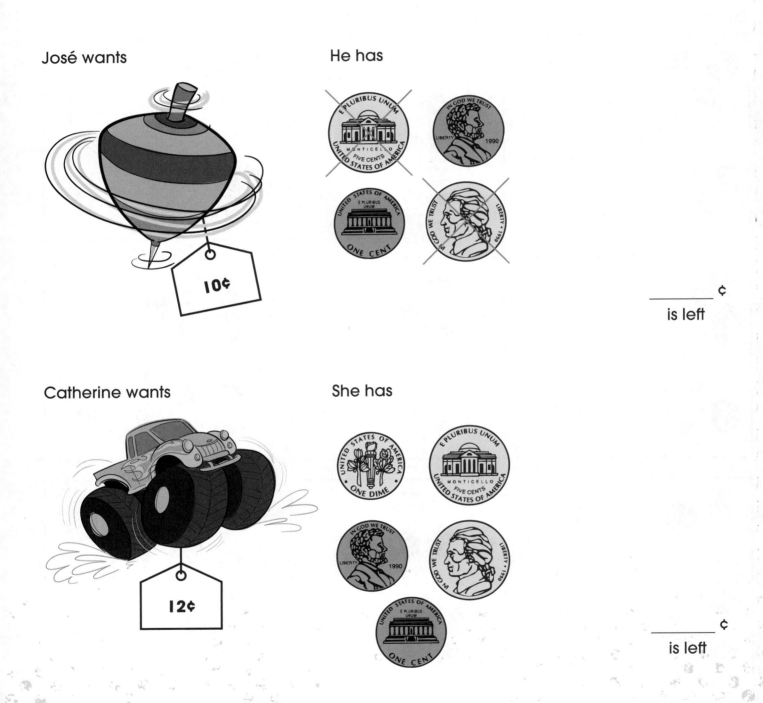

10¢

_____¢
is left

Catherine wants

She has

12¢

_____¢
is left

Subtracting with Dimes, Nickels, and Pennies

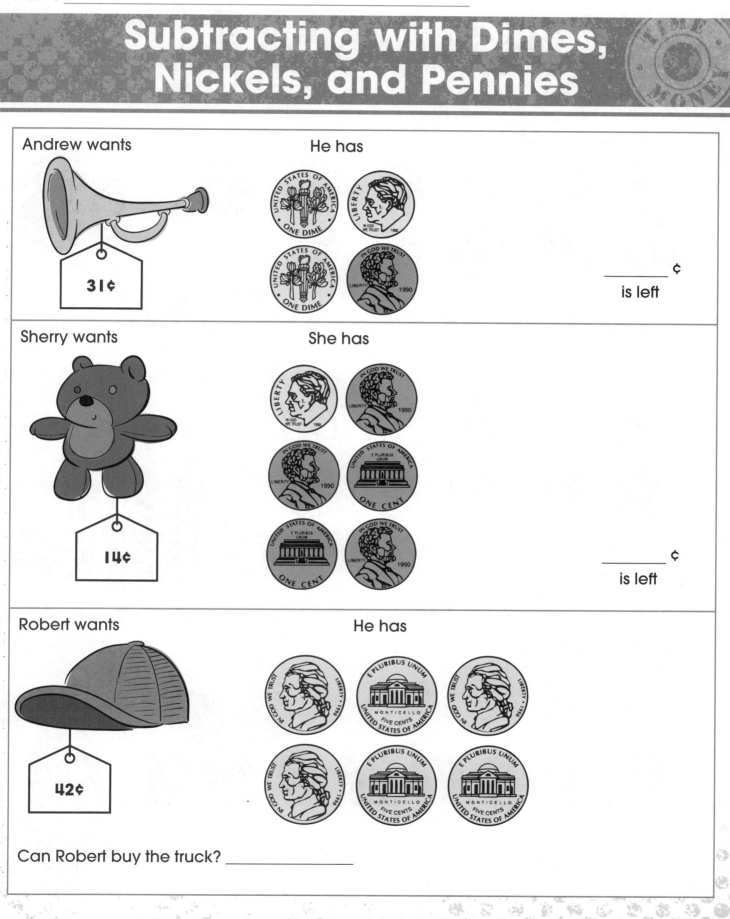

Andrew wants

He has

31¢

_____ ¢
is left

Sherry wants

She has

14¢

_____ ¢
is left

Robert wants

He has

42¢

Can Robert buy the truck? _____

Subtracting with Dimes, Nickels, and Pennies

Pay the exact amount for each toy.

A.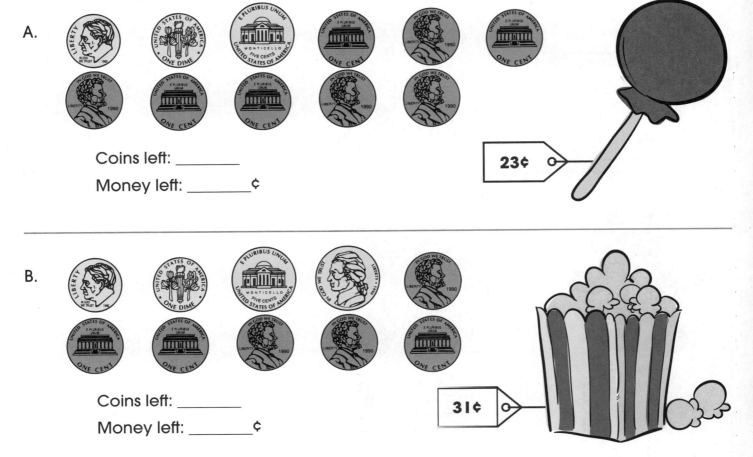

Coins left: _____

Money left: _____ ¢

23¢

B.

Coins left: _____

Money left: _____ ¢

31¢

C. Choose a price between 30¢ and 40¢.
Write the price on the tag.

Coins left: _____

Money left: _____

_____ ¢

Quarters: Introduction

Presenting... the quarter!

Our first president, George Washington, is on the front.

front   back

_____ quarter = _____ pennies

_____ quarter = _____ cents

_____ quarter = _____ ¢

Count these nickels by fives.

Is this another way to make 25¢?

yes   no

Quarters: Combinations of 25 Cents

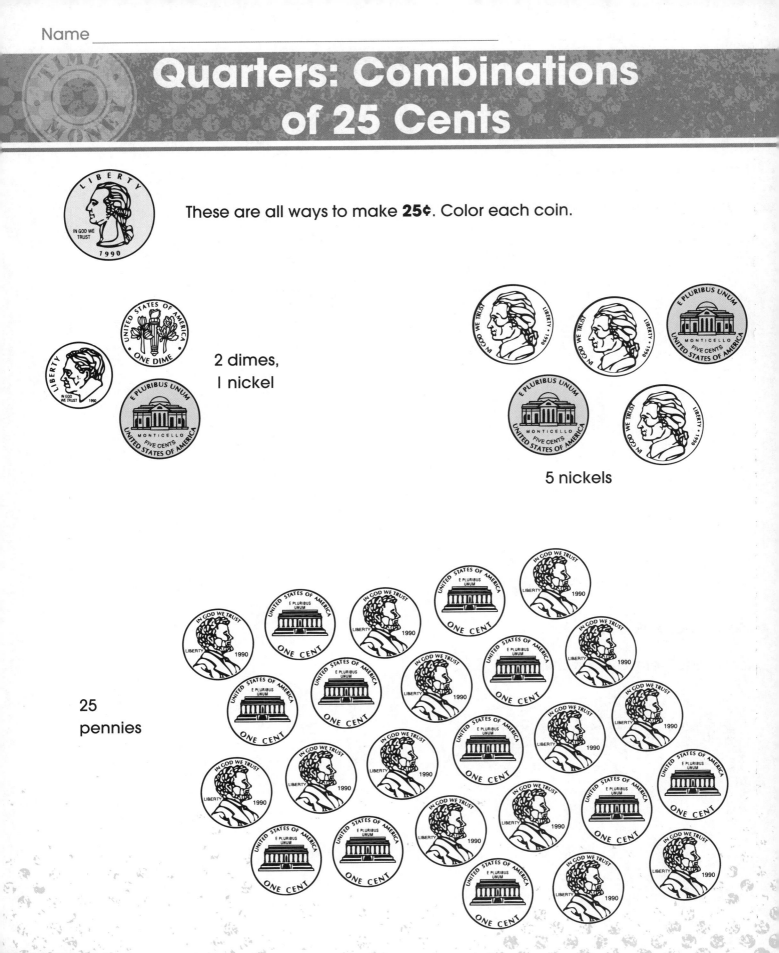

These are all ways to make **25¢**. Color each coin.

2 dimes,
1 nickel

5 nickels

25
pennies

Quarters: Combinations of 25 Cents

Count the money. Write the amount. A **quarter** is worth **25¢**.

A.

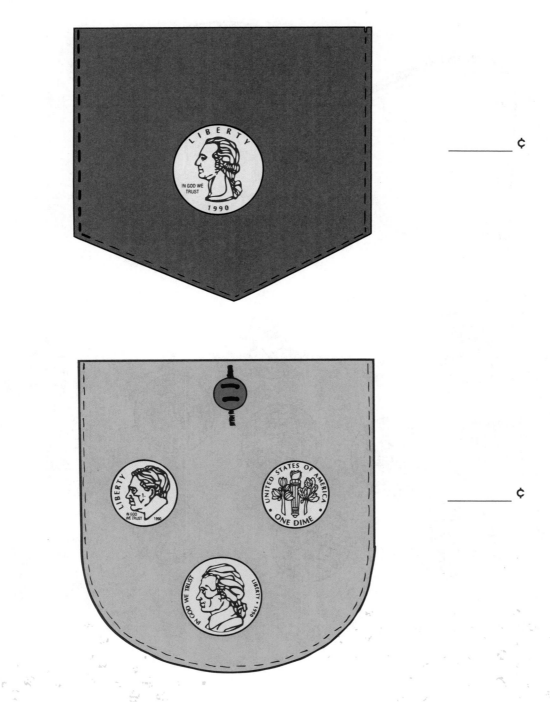

_____ ¢

B.

_____ ¢

Quarters: Combinations of 25 Cents

It costs 25¢ to catch a fish. Circle each group of coins that makes 25¢. How many fish can I catch?

Draw and color the fish I can catch.

Quarters: More or Less Than 50 Cents

The tooth fairy left 2 shiny quarters for your baby tooth.

How much money do you have?
Each quarter is worth 25¢. Two quarters = 50¢

Color each toy you can buy.

49¢

72¢

45¢

39¢

25¢

5¢

60¢

Quarters: More or Less Than 50 Cents

Some children had fun spending the allowance they earned. The boys bought some cars.

Tavaris paid 5¢ for each blue car. Color Tavaris's cars blue.

How much did Tavaris pay for the blue cars? _____ ¢

Lucas liked the red cars. They were the same price. Color his cars red.

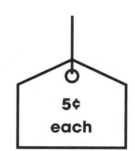

How much did Lucas pay for the red cars? _____ ¢

Which boy paid more? _____

Counting with Quarters

Some machines use quarters.

Color each machine you have to put quarters into. Circle the number of quarters you need.

I need _____ quarters to wash clothes.

I need _____ quarter(s) to make a phone call.

I need _____ quarters to buy a drink.

I need _____ quarters to buy a comic book.

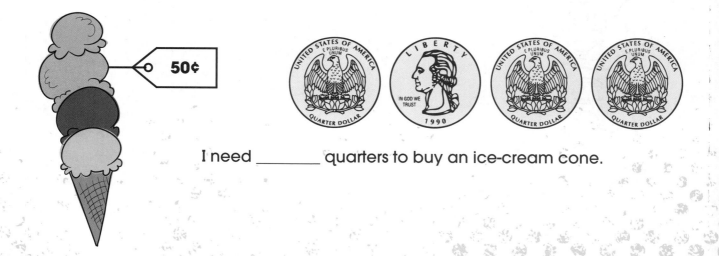

I need _____ quarters to buy an ice-cream cone.

Counting with Quarters, Dimes, Nickels, and Pennies

Count the money. Start with the quarters. Then count the dimes, nickels and pennies.

A.

_____ _____ _____ _____

Total

B.
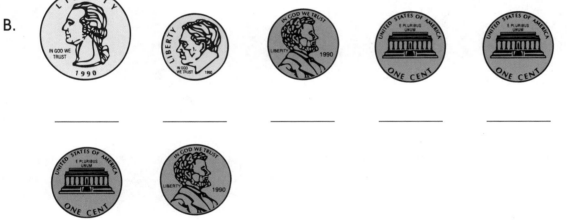

_____ _____ _____ _____ _____

_____ _____

Total

Counting with Quarters, Dimes, Nickels, and Pennies

Count the money. Write the amount. A quarter is worth 25¢.

A.

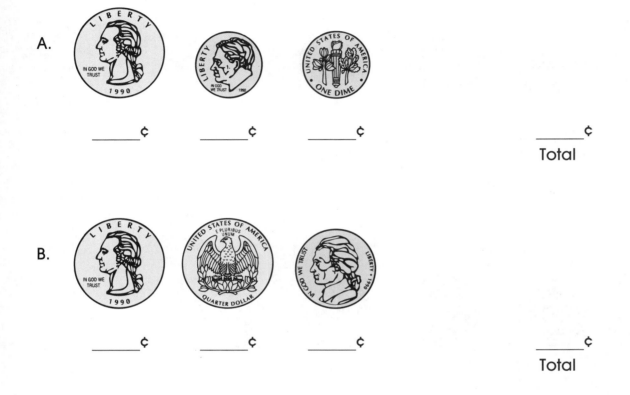

_____¢   _____¢   _____¢

_____¢
Total

B.

_____¢   _____¢   _____¢

_____¢
Total

C.   Put more than 50¢ in the bank. Show the coins.

_____¢
Total

Counting with Quarters, Dimes, Nickels, and Pennies

Count the money. Start with the quarters. Then count the dimes, nickels and pennies.

A. _____ ¢   _____ ¢   _____ ¢   _____ ¢   _____ ¢
                                                    Total

B. _____ ¢   _____ ¢   _____ ¢   _____ ¢   _____ ¢   _____ ¢

_____ ¢   _____ ¢
          Total

C. Solve this puzzle.
    What coins does Dinosaur have?

I'm counting
my money.
25¢, 35¢, 45¢, 55¢,
60¢, 65¢, 66¢, 67¢

Counting with Quarters, Dimes, Nickels, and Pennies

Count the money. Start with the quarter. Write the amount.

A.

_____ ¢

B.

_____ ¢

Counting with Quarters, Dimes, Nickels, and Pennies

Match the money with the amount.

35¢

36¢

40¢

27¢

15¢

21¢

8¢

Counting with Quarters, Dimes, Nickels, and Pennies

Count the coins. Do you have enough money to buy each toy?

Example:

You have...

yes or no

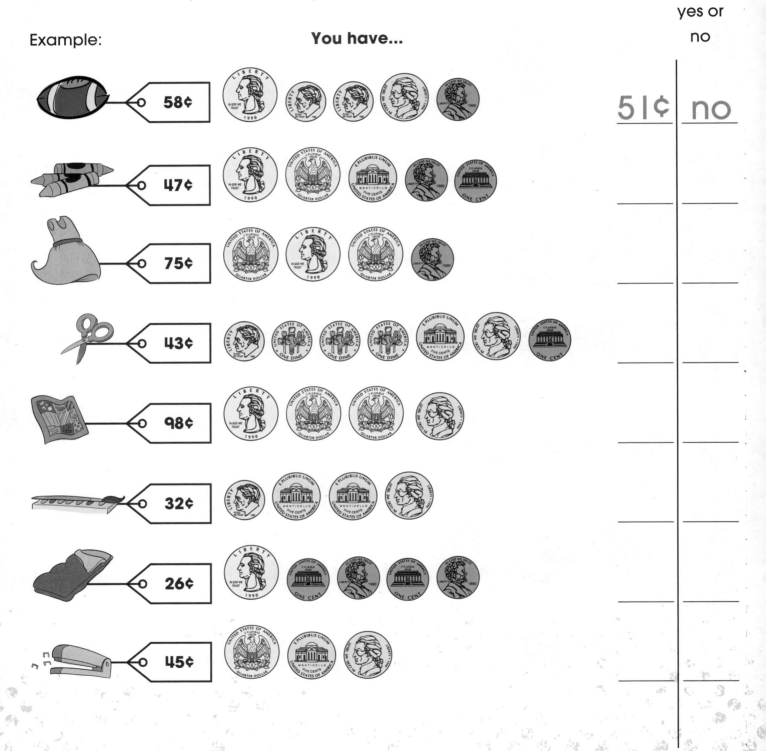

58¢	51¢ no
47¢	
75¢	
43¢	
98¢	
32¢	
26¢	
45¢	

Counting with Quarters, Dimes, Nickels, and Pennies

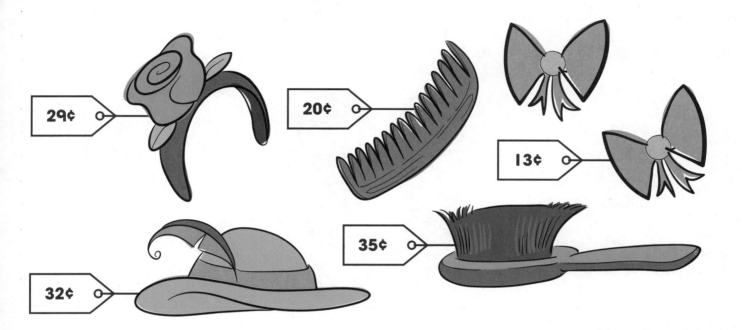

How many of each coin do you need to buy each item? Write 0, 1, 2, 3 or 4.

	Quarters	Dimes	Nickels	Pennies

Subtracting for Change

Adam wanted to know how much change he would have left when he bought things.

He made a picture to help him subtract.

4 dimes		40¢
− 1 dime		− 10¢
3 dimes		30¢

Cross out and subtract.

6 dimes		60¢
− 4 dime		− 40¢
dimes		

Subtracting for Change

Pay the exact amount for each toy. Cross out the coins you use.

How much is left?

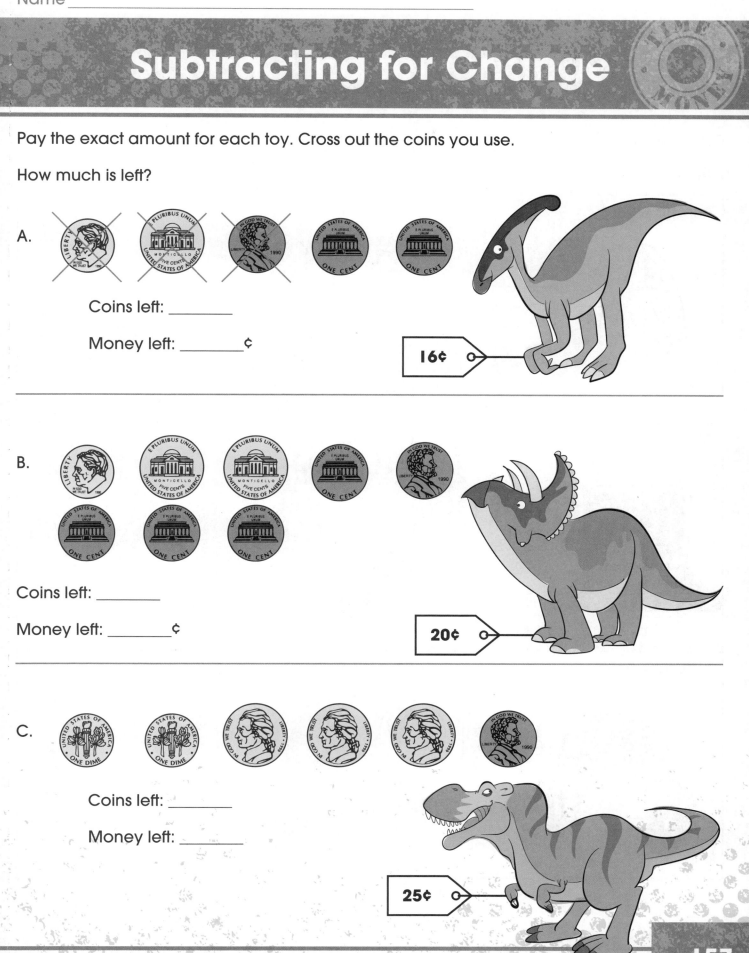

A.

Coins left: _____

Money left: _____ ¢

16¢

B.

Coins left: _____

Money left: _____ ¢

20¢

C.

Coins left: _____

Money left: _____

25¢

Subtracting for Change

Cross out the coins you use. Write the problem.

Example:

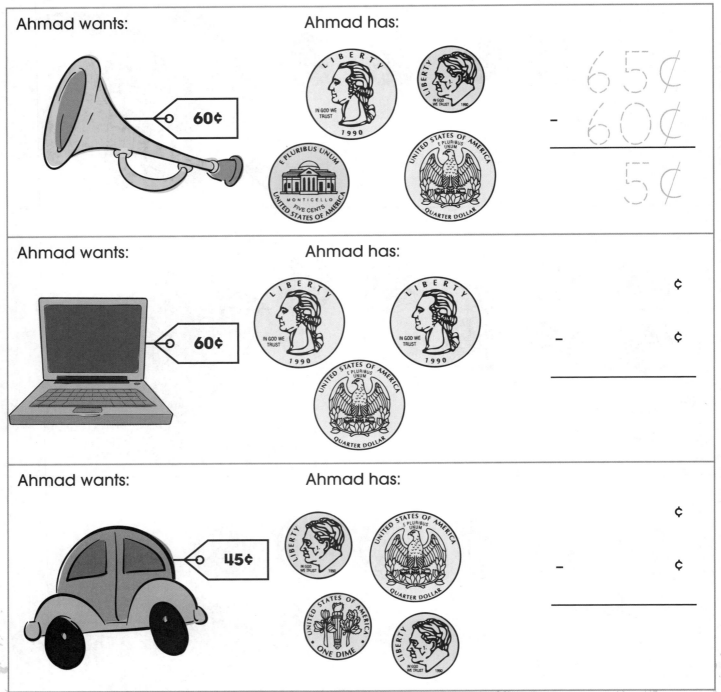

Ahmad wants:

60¢

Ahmad has:

65¢
-60¢
___
5¢

Ahmad wants:

60¢

Ahmad has:

___¢
-___¢
_____

Ahmad wants:

45¢

Ahmad has:

___¢
-___¢
_____

Subtracting from 50 Cents

Maria went to the store to buy a birthday gift for her best friend. Maria took 50¢ to the store.

Circle the things she could buy.

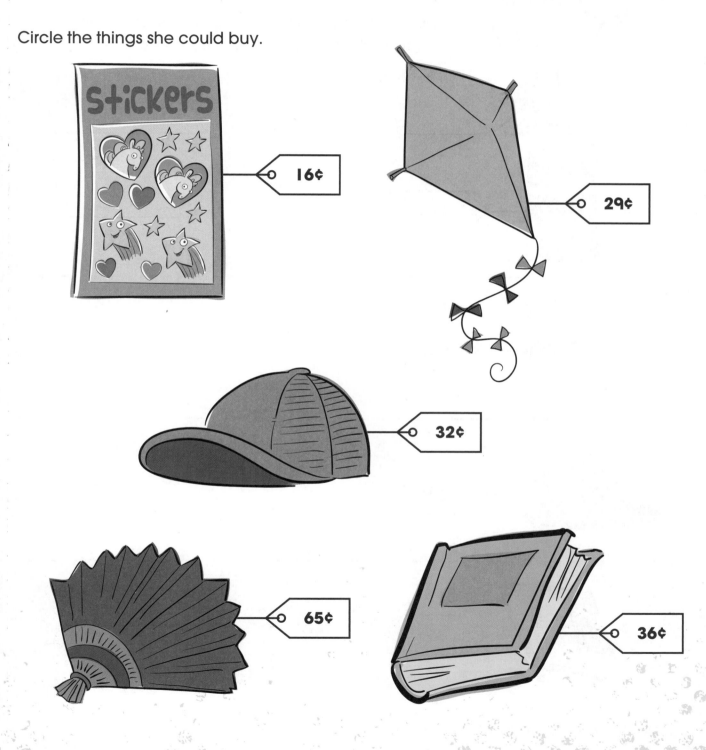

Subtracting from 50 Cents

Maria had 50¢. She wanted to know how much change she would get back from each toy.

stickers

16¢

50¢
–   ¢
_____

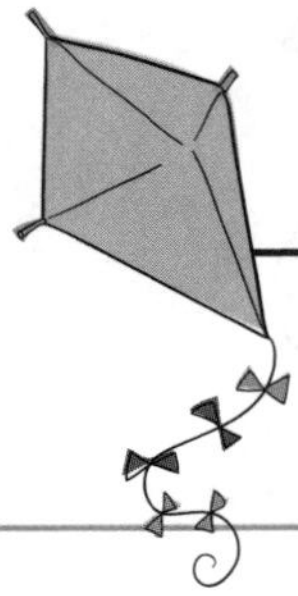

29¢

50¢
–   ¢
_____

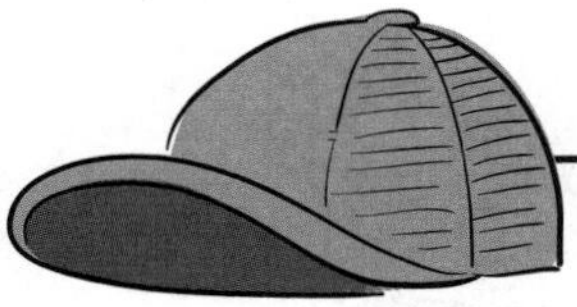

32¢

50¢
–   ¢
_____

36¢

50¢
–   ¢
_____

Color the toy you think Maria chose.

Making Exact Amounts of Money

Use dimes, nickels and pennies. Pay the exact amount for each toy.

A.   What coins did you use?

_____ dimes   _____ nickels

_____ pennies

B.   What coins did you use?

_____ dimes   _____ nickels

_____ pennies

C.   Solve this puzzle.

What coins did Cat
use to pay for the ball?

_____ dimes   _____ nickels

_____ pennies

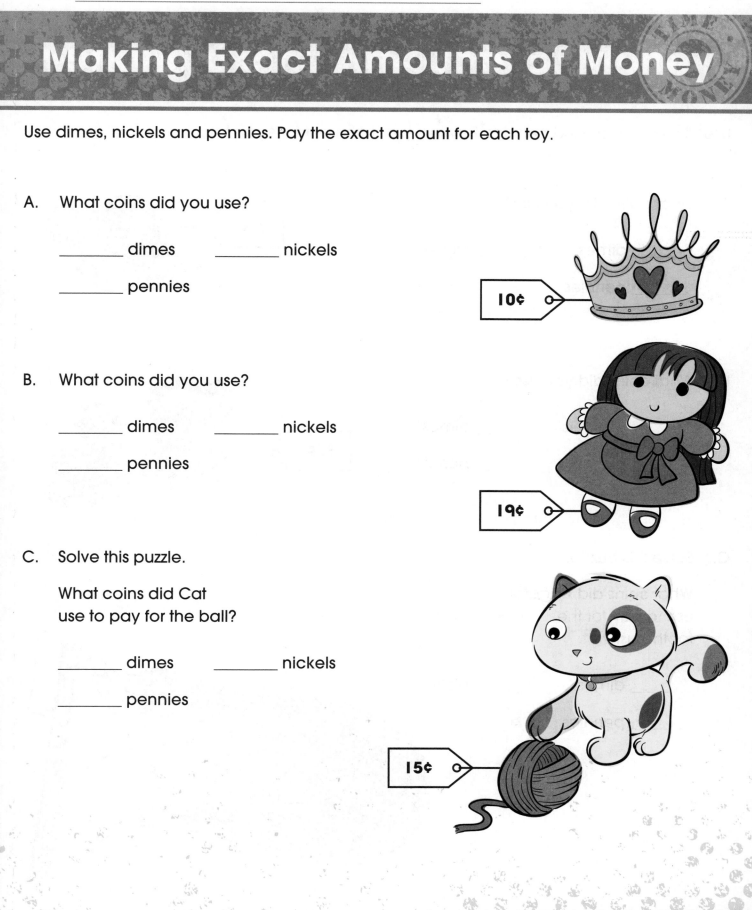

10¢

19¢

15¢

Making Exact Amounts of Money

Use dimes, nickels and pennies. Pay the exact amount for each toy.

A. What coins did you use?

_____ dimes   _____ nickels

_____ pennies

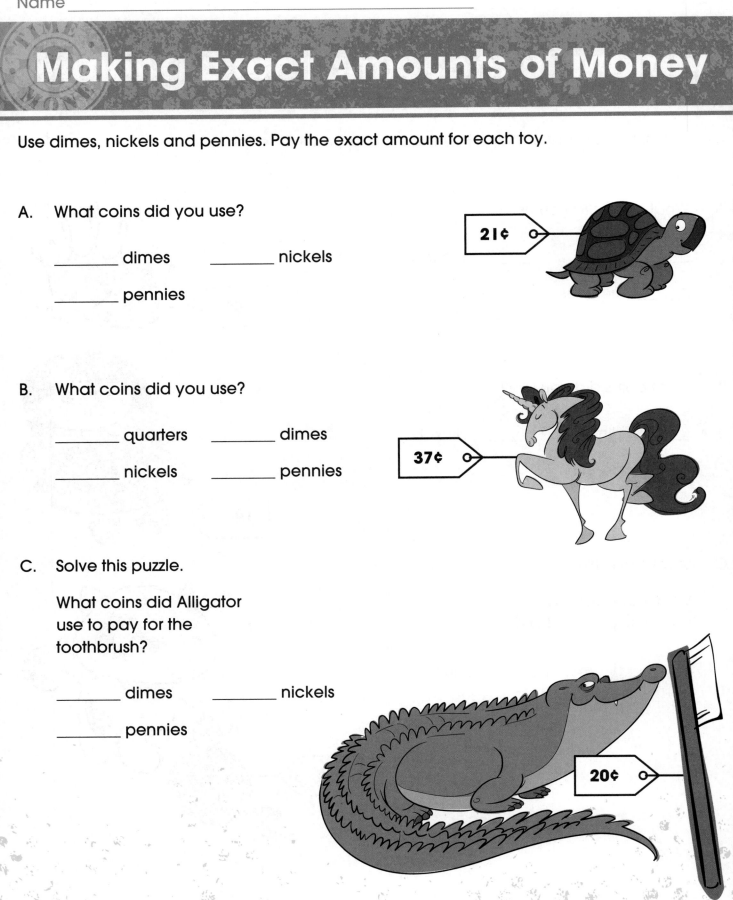

21¢

B. What coins did you use?

_____ quarters   _____ dimes

_____ nickels   _____ pennies

37¢

C. Solve this puzzle.

What coins did Alligator
use to pay for the
toothbrush?

_____ dimes   _____ nickels

_____ pennies

20¢

Making Exact Amounts of Money

Use quarters, dimes, nickels and pennies. Pay the exact amount for each toy.

A. What coins did you use?

_____ quarters   _____ dimes

_____ nickels   _____ pennies

27¢

B. What coins did you use?

_____ quarters   _____ dimes

_____ nickels   _____ pennies

40¢

C. Solve this puzzle.

What coins did Cat use
to pay for the hair bows?

_____ quarters   _____ dimes

_____ nickels   _____ pennies

30¢

Name _____

Making Exact Amounts of Money and Change

Use the coins shown. Pay the exact amount for each toy.

How much do you have left?

A.

Coins left: _____

Money left: _____ ¢

37 ¢

B.

Coins left: _____

Money left: _____ ¢

50¢

C.

Choose a price between 42¢ and
58¢. Write the price on the tag.

Coins left: _____

Money left: _____ ¢

¢

Name _____

Use the coins shown. Pay the exact amount for each toy.

A.

Coins left: _____

Money left: _____ ¢

48¢

B.

Coins left: _____

Money left: _____ ¢

53¢

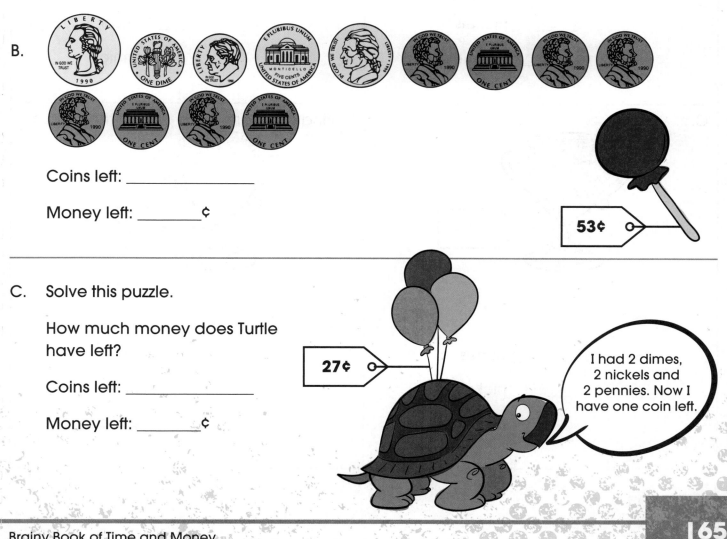

C.   Solve this puzzle.

How much money does Turtle have left?

27¢

I had 2 dimes, 2 nickels and 2 pennies. Now I have one coin left.

Coins left: _____

Money left: _____ ¢

Problem Solving with Money

Draw the coins you use. Write the number of coins on each blank.

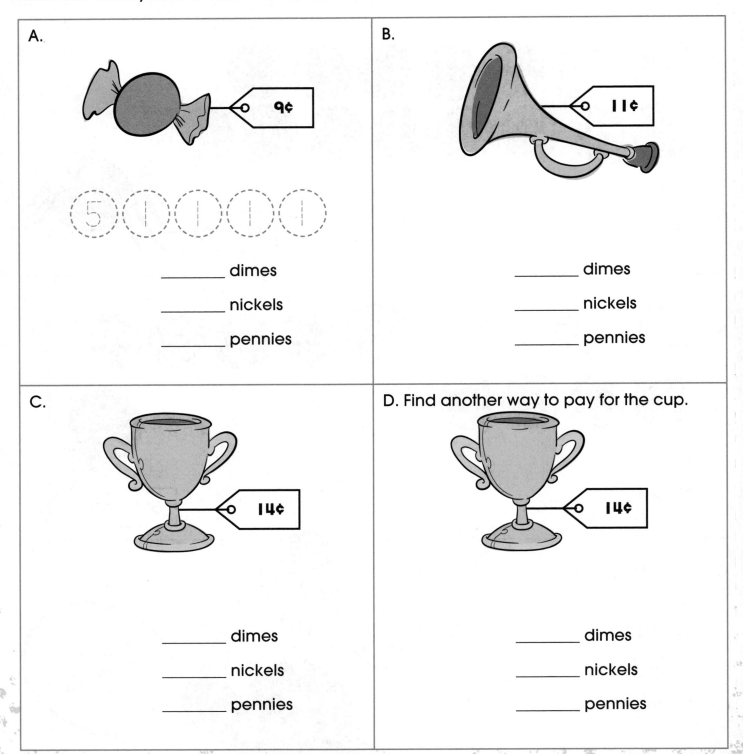

A.

9¢

_____ dimes

_____ nickels

_____ pennies

B.

11¢

_____ dimes

_____ nickels

_____ pennies

C.

14¢

_____ dimes

_____ nickels

_____ pennies

D. Find another way to pay for the cup.

14¢

_____ dimes

_____ nickels

_____ pennies

Problem Solving with Money

Draw the coins you use. Write the number of coins on each blank.

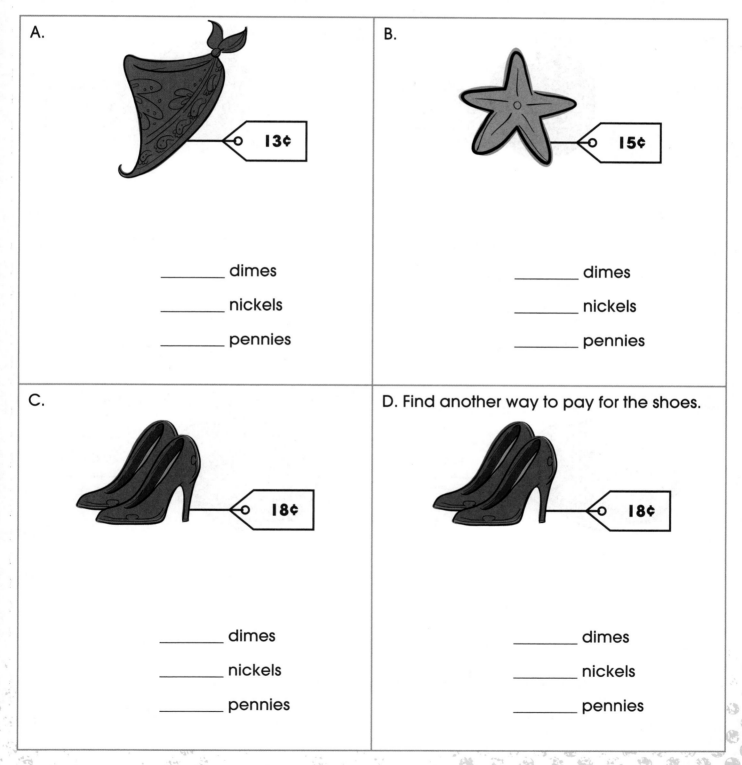

A.

13¢

_____ dimes

_____ nickels

_____ pennies

B.

15¢

_____ dimes

_____ nickels

_____ pennies

C.

18¢

_____ dimes

_____ nickels

_____ pennies

D. Find another way to pay for the shoes.

18¢

_____ dimes

_____ nickels

_____ pennies

Problem Solving with Money

Draw the coins you use. Write the number of coins on each blank.

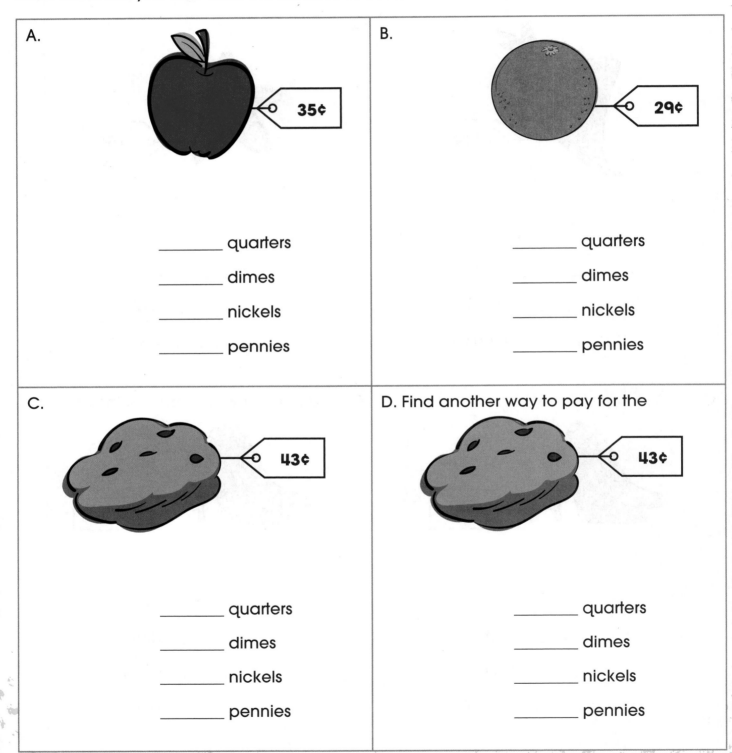

A.

35¢

_____ quarters

_____ dimes

_____ nickels

_____ pennies

B.

29¢

_____ quarters

_____ dimes

_____ nickels

_____ pennies

C.

43¢

_____ quarters

_____ dimes

_____ nickels

_____ pennies

D. Find another way to pay for the

43¢

_____ quarters

_____ dimes

_____ nickels

_____ pennies

Making Exact Amounts of Money: Two Ways to Pay

Find two ways to pay. Show what coins you use.

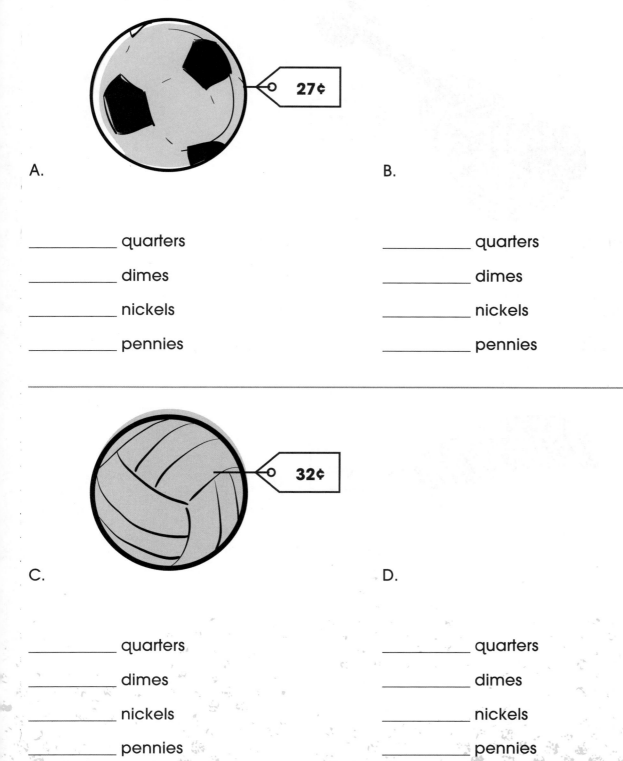

A.

_____ quarters

_____ dimes

_____ nickels

_____ pennies

B.

_____ quarters

_____ dimes

_____ nickels

_____ pennies

C.

_____ quarters

_____ dimes

_____ nickels

_____ pennies

D.

_____ quarters

_____ dimes

_____ nickels

_____ pennies

Making Exact Amounts of Money: Two Ways to Pay

Find two ways to pay. Show what coins you use.

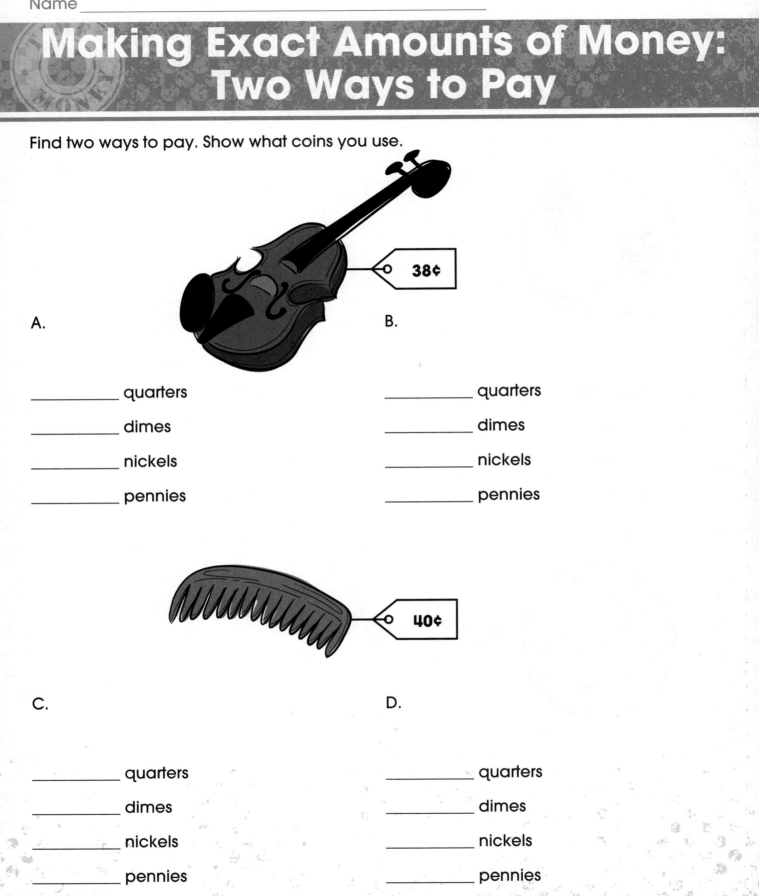

38¢

A.

_____ quarters

_____ dimes

_____ nickels

_____ pennies

B.

_____ quarters

_____ dimes

_____ nickels

_____ pennies

40¢

C.

_____ quarters

_____ dimes

_____ nickels

_____ pennies

D.

_____ quarters

_____ dimes

_____ nickels

_____ pennies

Making Exact Amounts of Money: How Much More?

Count the coins. Find out how much more money you need to pay the exact amount.

A.

How much money do you have? _____ ¢

How much more money do you need? _____ ¢

25¢

B.

How much money do you have? _____ ¢

How much more money do you need? _____ ¢

45¢

C.   Solve this puzzle.

How much more
money does
Frog need?

_____ ¢

I have
1 quarter,
2 nickels, and
15 pennies.
I need one more
coin to buy
the crayon.

55¢

Making Exact Amounts of Money: How Much More?

Count the coins. Find out how much more money you need to pay the exact amount.

A.

How much money do you have? _____ ¢

How much more money do you need? _____ ¢

50¢

B.

How much money do you have? _____ ¢

How much more money do you need? _____ ¢

60¢

C. Solve this puzzle.

How much more money does Monkey need?

_____ ¢

I have 1 quarter and 4 dimes. I need one more coin to pay for the banana.

75¢

Half-Dollars: Introduction

Meet the half-dollar!

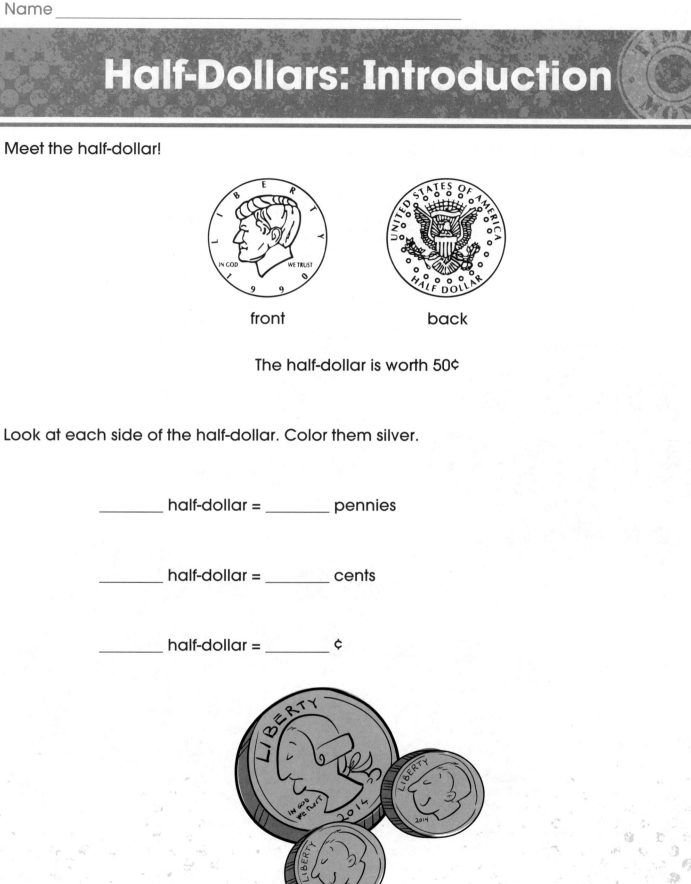

front   back

The half-dollar is worth 50¢

Look at each side of the half-dollar. Color them silver.

_____ half-dollar = _____ pennies

_____ half-dollar = _____ cents

_____ half-dollar = _____ ¢

These are some ways to make a half dollar. Color each coin.

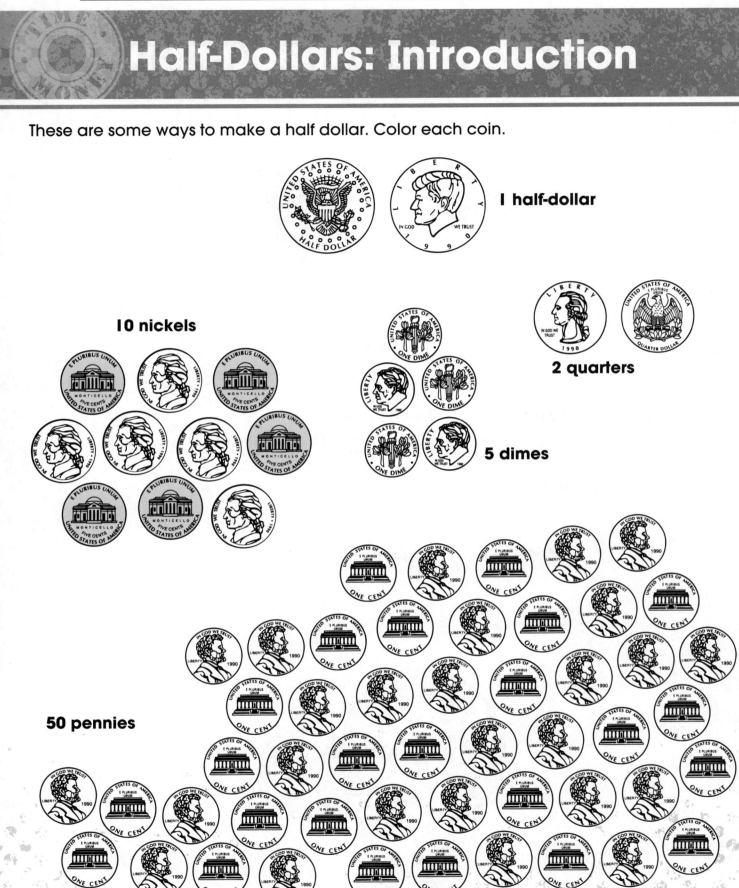

1 half-dollar

10 nickels

2 quarters

5 dimes

50 pennies

Counting Half-Dollars, Quarters, Dimes, Nickels, and Pennies

Count the money. Write each amount. A half-dollar is worth **50¢** or **$.50**.

A.

_____   _____   _____   _____¢
                                              Total

B.

_____   _____   _____   _____   _____¢
                                                  Total

C.   Draw between 50¢ and 90¢ in the jar.

Counting Half-Dollars, Quarters, Dimes, Nickels, and Pennies

Count the money. Write each amount.

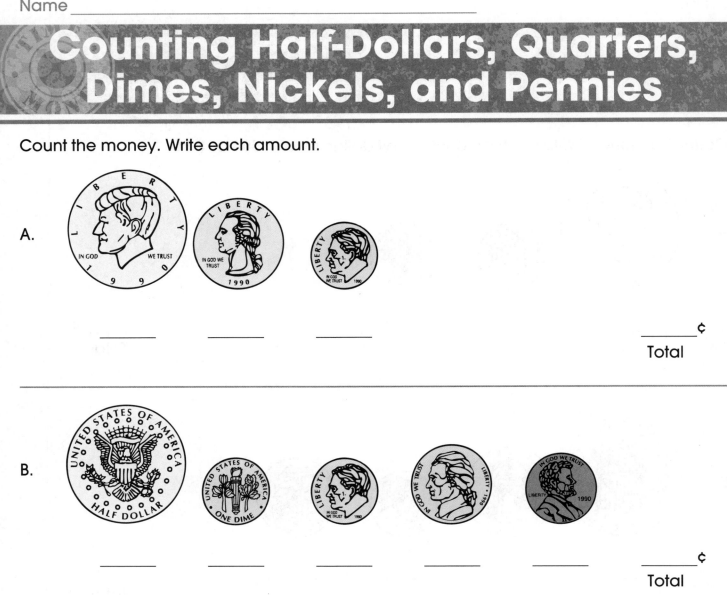

A.

_____ _____ _____

_____ ¢
Total

B.

_____ _____ _____ _____ _____

_____ ¢
Total

C.   Draw more than 80¢ in the pocket.

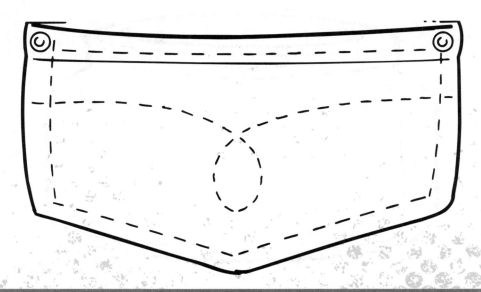

Counting Coins: How Much More?

Count the coins. Find out how much more money you need to pay the exact amount.

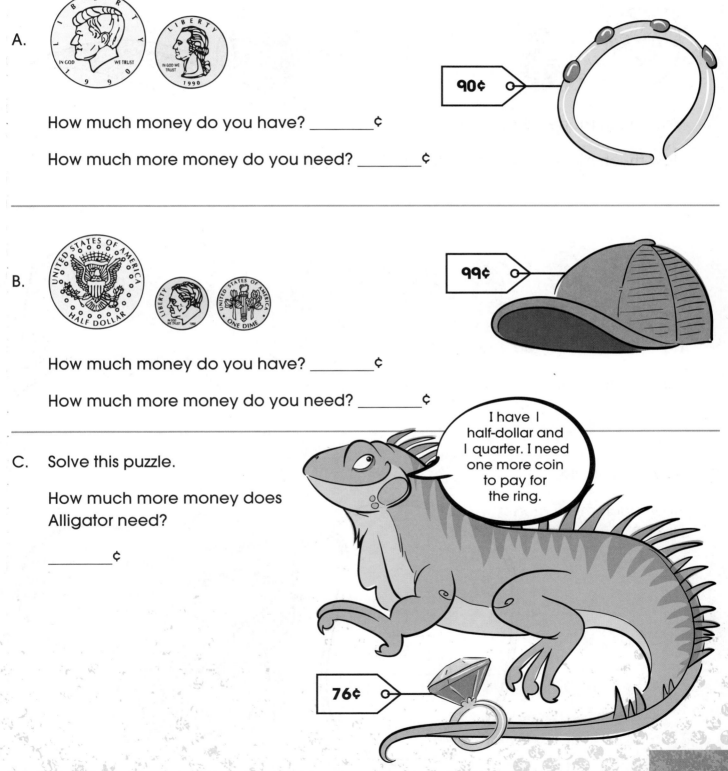

A.

How much money do you have? _____¢

How much more money do you need? _____¢

90¢

B.

How much money do you have? _____¢

How much more money do you need? _____¢

99¢

C. Solve this puzzle.

How much more money does
Alligator need?

_____¢

I have I half-dollar and I quarter. I need one more coin to pay for the ring.

76¢

Counting Coins: How Much More?

Count the coins. Find out how much more money you need to pay the exact amount.

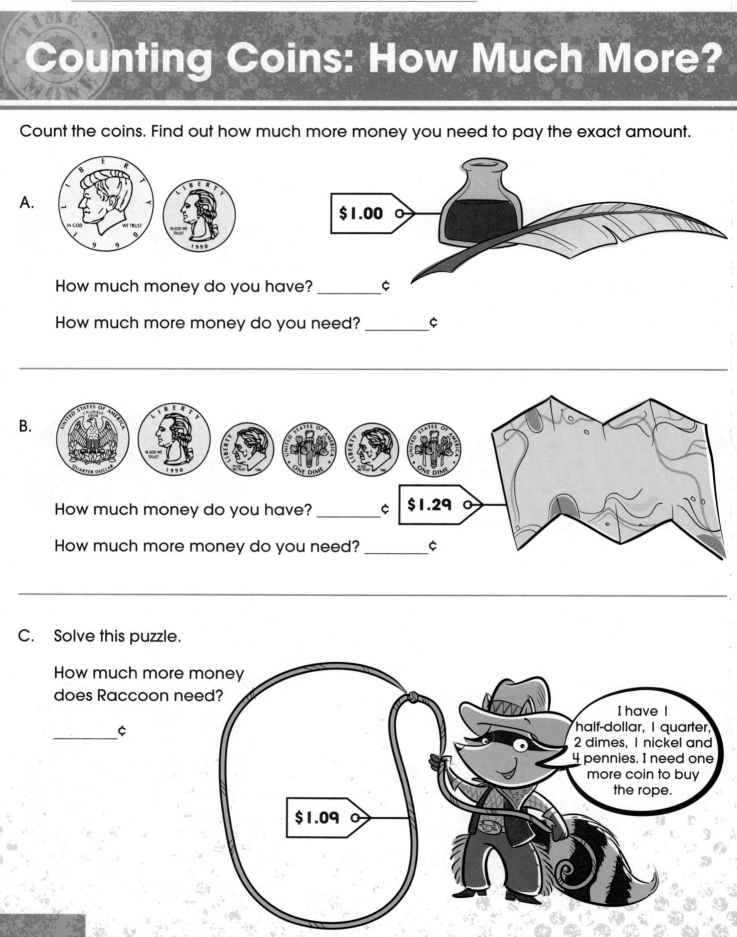

A.

How much money do you have? _____ ¢

How much more money do you need? _____ ¢

B.

How much money do you have? _____ ¢ $1.29

How much more money do you need? _____ ¢

C. Solve this puzzle.

How much more money
does Raccoon need?

_____ ¢

I have 1 half-dollar, 1 quarter, 2 dimes, 1 nickel and 4 pennies. I need one more coin to buy the rope.

$1.09

Dollar Bills: Introduction

This is a **dollar bill**.

It has **2 sides**.

Color them green.

1 dollar = $1.00

1 dollar = <u>one dollar</u>

1 dollar = <u>100</u> pennies

1 dollar = <u>100</u> cents

This is the **dollar sign**: **$**
It is an S with a line through it.

There is also a period between the dollars and the cents: $1.00

Name _____

Here are some more ways to make a dollar!

Count each set of coins. If it equals one dollar, write $1.00 on the line.

Count by tens with dimes. _____

Count by fives with nickels. _____

It is a lot easier to carry **1 dollar bill** than **20 nickels!**

Counting with Dollar Bills and Coins

A few **dollar tips** for you...

    1. Drop the ¢ sign.

    2. Add the $ sign.

    3. Use a . (period) between the dollars and cents.

Write the amount of dollars and cents.

1.

$ 1.08

2.

$ _____

Counting with Dollar Bills and Coins

Count the money. Write each amount.

A one-dollar bill ~~image~~ is worth 100¢ or $1.00

A. _____ _____ $ 1.25

B. _____ _____ _____ $_____

C. Draw about $2.00 in the bank. Use a one-dollar bill.

Matching Dollar Amounts

Count the money. Draw a line to match.

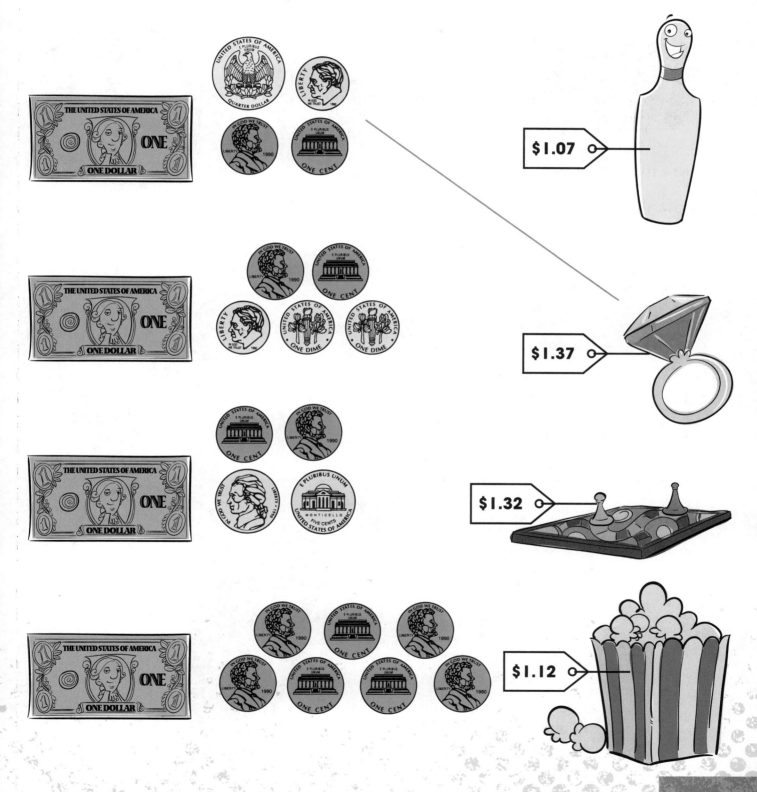

$1.07

$1.37

$1.32

$1.12

Name _____

Count the coins and bills. Find out how much more money you need to pay the exact amount.

A.

$1.67

How much money do you have? $_____

How much more money do you need? _____¢

B.

$1.75

How much money do you have? $_____

How much more money do you need? _____¢

C. Solve this puzzle.

How much more money does Anteater need?

_____¢

I have 1 dollar bill, 1 quarter, 1 dime, and 1 penny. I need one more coin to buy the clipboard.

$1.61

Estimating Amounts of Money

We estimate, or round up or down, to make a quick guess about money.

Circle the amount that is closer to the amount on the tag. **This is an estimate.**

about 40¢

about 30¢

39¢

about 30¢

about 40¢

38¢

about 30¢

about 40¢

about 40¢

42¢

Estimating Amounts of Money

Circle the best estimate.

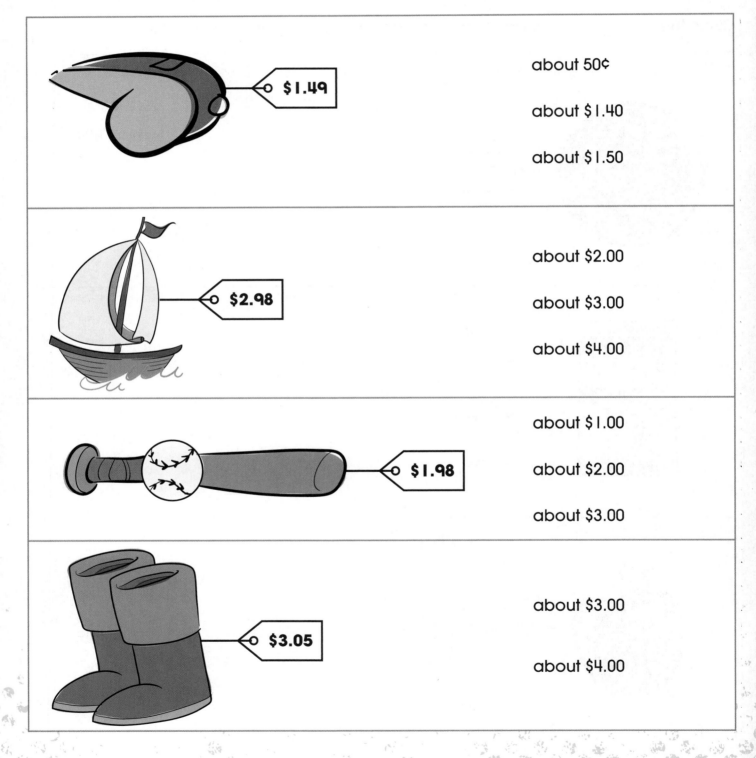

$1.49

about 50¢

about $1.40

about $1.50

$2.98

about $2.00

about $3.00

about $4.00

$1.98

about $1.00

about $2.00

about $3.00

$3.05

about $3.00

about $4.00

Adding and Subtracting Amounts of Money: Using Estimation

Using estimation makes it much easier to add or subtract in your head.

These foods are for sale in the lunchroom.

39¢   21¢   19¢   11¢   29¢

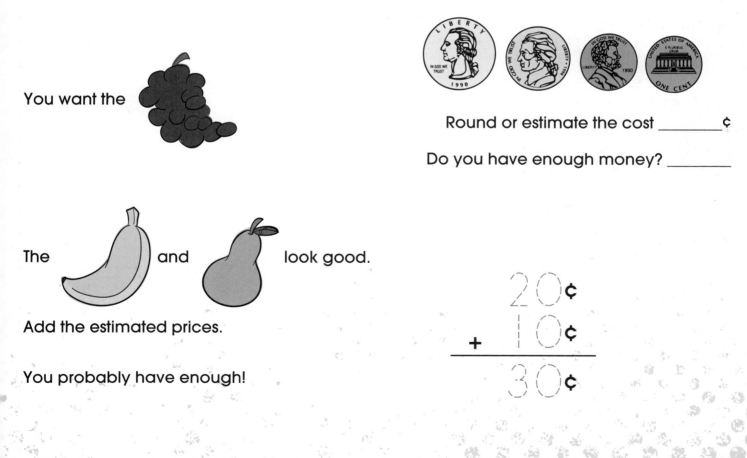

You have this much money:

You want the

Round or estimate the cost _____ ¢

Do you have enough money? _____

The ⟨banana⟩ and ⟨pear⟩ look good.

Add the estimated prices.

You probably have enough!

$$
\begin{array}{r}
20¢ \\
+\ 10¢ \\
\hline
30¢ \\
\end{array}
$$

Adding and Subtracting Amounts of Money: Using Estimation

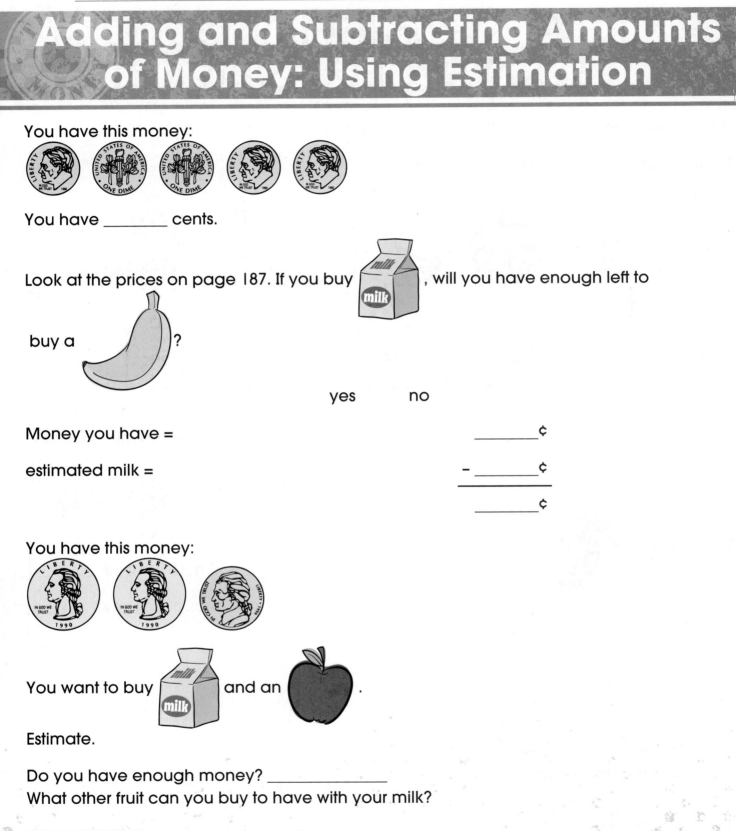

You have this money:

You have _____ cents.

Look at the prices on page 187. If you buy [milk], will you have enough left to

buy a [banana]?

yes   no

Money you have =   _____ ¢

estimated milk =   – _____ ¢
                                                    _____ ¢

You have this money:

You want to buy [milk] and an [apple].

Estimate.

Do you have enough money? _____
What other fruit can you buy to have with your milk?

_____

Adding and Subtracting Amounts of Money: Making Change

How much change should you get?

Example:

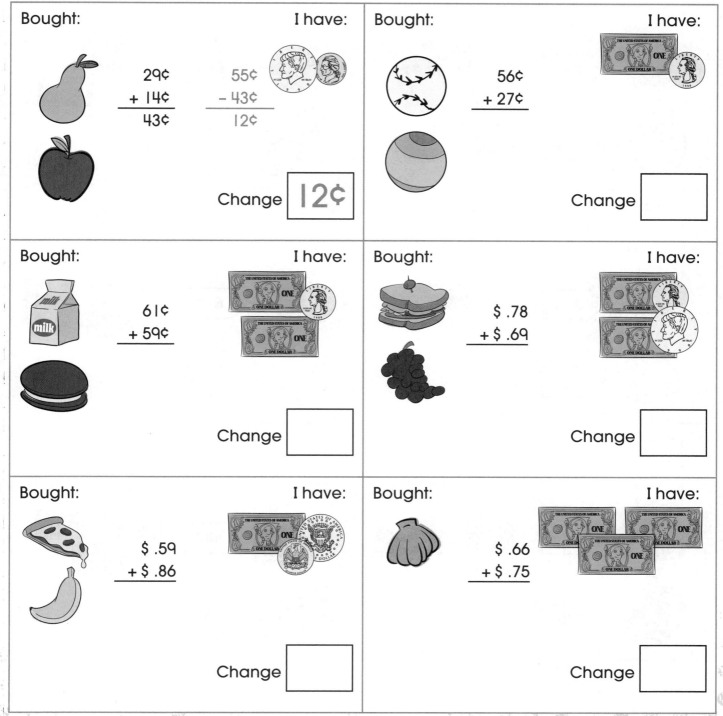

Bought:

29¢
+ 14¢
43¢

I have: 55¢

– 43¢
12¢

Change 12¢

Bought:

56¢
+ 27¢

I have:

Change

Bought:

61¢
+ 59¢

I have:

Change

Bought:

$ .78
+ $ .69

I have:

Change

Bought:

$ .59
+ $ .86

I have:

Change

Bought:

$ .66
+ $ .75

I have:

Change

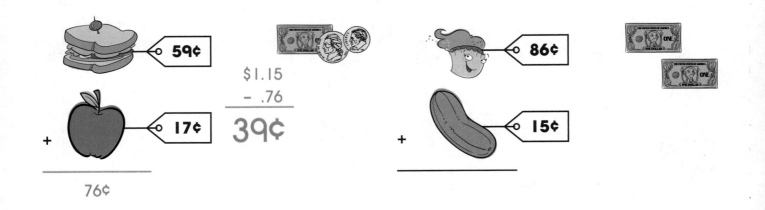

59¢

17¢

+

_____

76¢

$1.15
− .76
39¢

86¢

15¢

+

_____

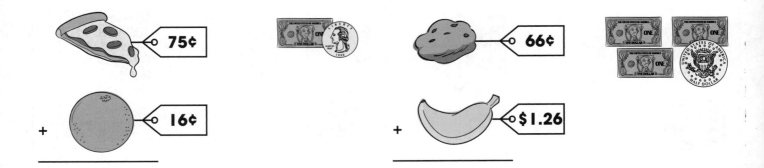

75¢

16¢

+

_____

66¢

$1.26

+

_____

77¢

54¢

+

_____

64¢

89¢

+

_____

Making Change: Money Puzzles

Solve the puzzles. Show how much change you get.

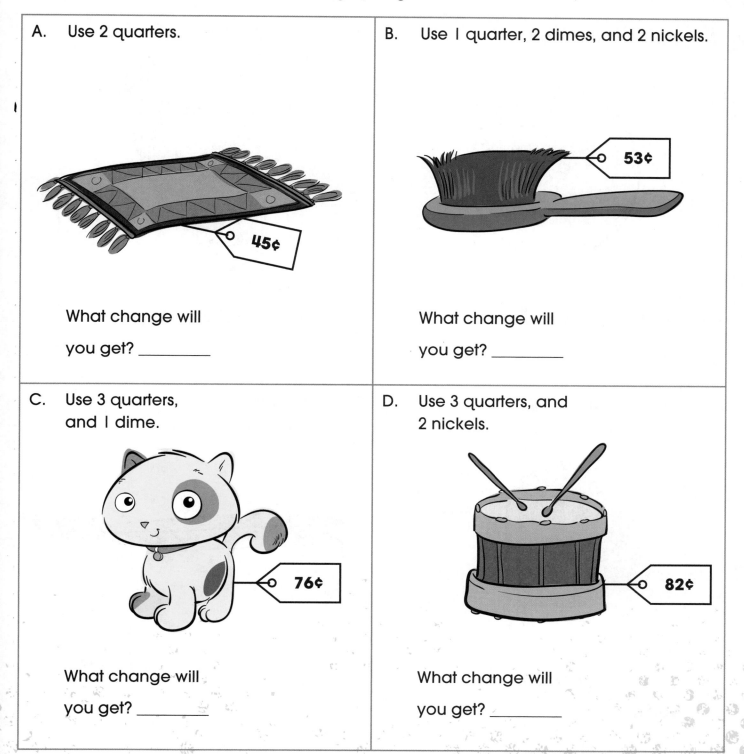

A. Use 2 quarters.

45¢

What change will
you get? _____

B. Use 1 quarter, 2 dimes, and 2 nickels.

53¢

What change will
you get? _____

C. Use 3 quarters,
and 1 dime.

76¢

What change will
you get? _____

D. Use 3 quarters, and
2 nickels.

82¢

What change will
you get? _____

Making Change: Money Puzzles

Solve the puzzles. Show how much change you get.

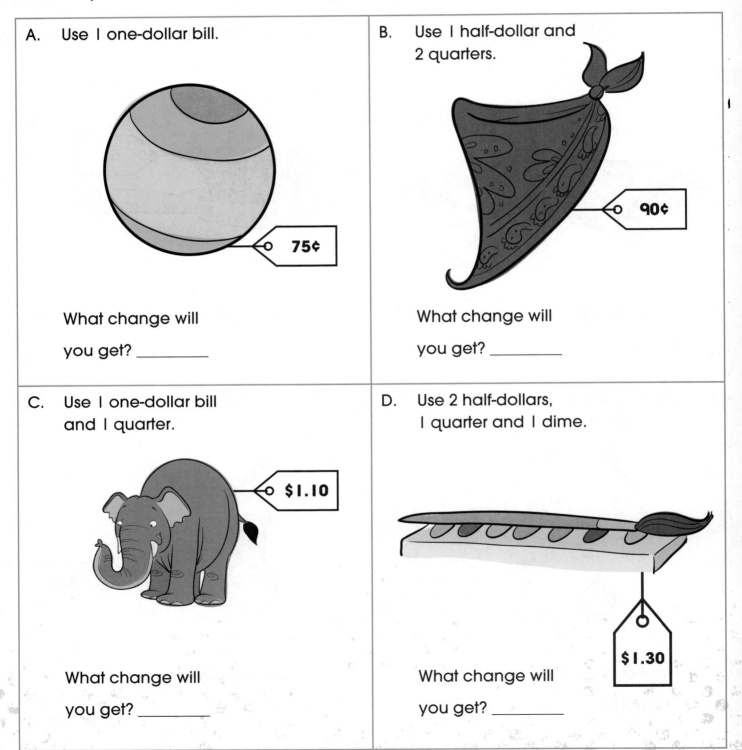

A. Use 1 one-dollar bill.

75¢

What change will
you get? _____

B. Use 1 half-dollar and
2 quarters.

90¢

What change will
you get? _____

C. Use 1 one-dollar bill
and 1 quarter.

$1.10

What change will
you get? _____

D. Use 2 half-dollars,
1 quarter and 1 dime.

$1.30

What change will
you get? _____

Making Change: Money Puzzles

Solve the puzzles. Show how much change you get.

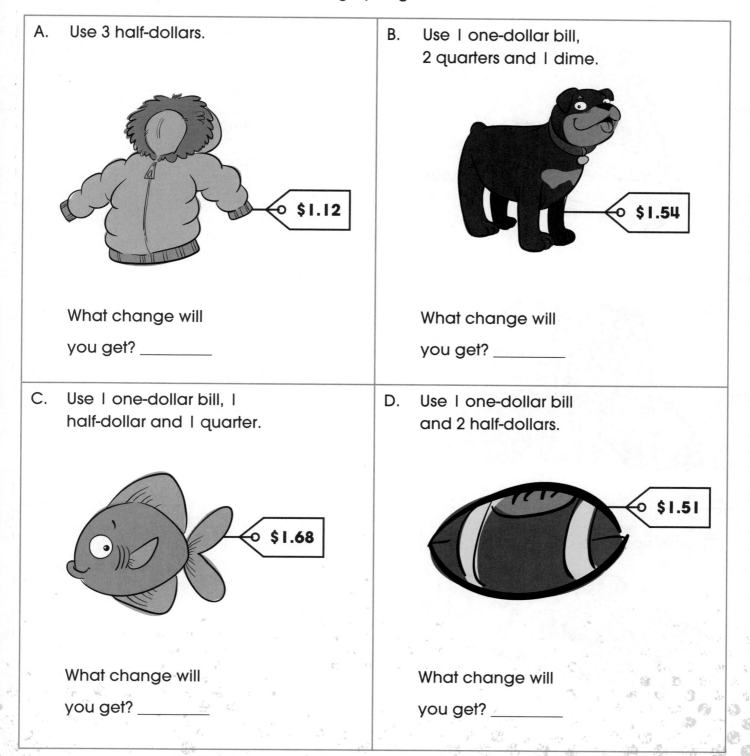

A.   Use 3 half-dollars.

$1.12

What change will

you get? _____

B.   Use 1 one-dollar bill,
      2 quarters and 1 dime.

$1.54

What change will

you get? _____

C.   Use 1 one-dollar bill, 1
      half-dollar and 1 quarter.

$1.68

What change will

you get? _____

D.   Use 1 one-dollar bill
      and 2 half-dollars.

$1.51

What change will

you get? _____

Making Exact Amounts of Money

Pay for each item. Show what coins you use.

A.

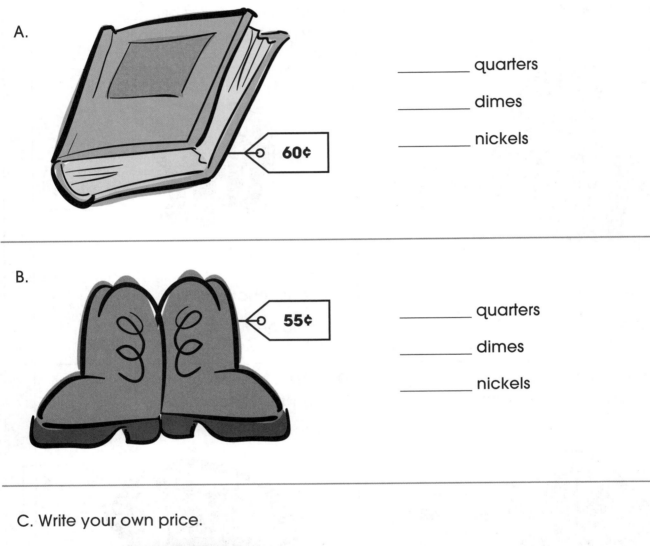

_____ quarters

_____ dimes

_____ nickels

60¢

B.

55¢

_____ quarters

_____ dimes

_____ nickels

C. Write your own price.

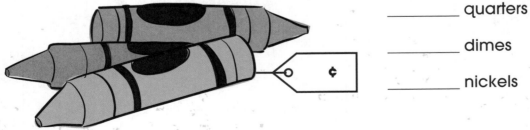

_____ quarters

_____ dimes

_____ nickels

¢

Making Exact Amounts of Money

Pay for each snack. Show what coins you use.

A.

65¢

_____ quarters

_____ dimes

_____ nickels

_____ pennies

B.

Corn Chips

49¢

_____ quarters

_____ dimes

_____ nickels

_____ pennies

C. Write your own price.

¢

_____ quarters

_____ dimes

_____ nickels

_____ pennies

Making Exact Amounts of Money

Pay for each robot. Show what coins you use.

A.

 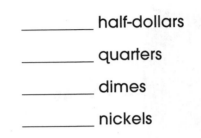

85¢

_____ half-dollars

_____ quarters

_____ dimes

_____ nickels

_____ pennies

B.

$1.00

_____ half-dollars

_____ quarters

_____ dimes

_____ nickels

_____ pennies

C. Write your own price.

 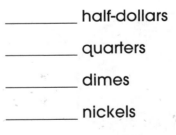

_____ half-dollars

_____ quarters

_____ dimes

_____ nickels

_____ pennies

Making Exact Amounts of Money

Pay for each toy. Show what coins you use.

A.

$1.50

_____ half-dollars

_____ quarters

_____ dimes

_____ nickels

_____ pennies

B.

$1.35

_____ half-dollars

_____ quarters

_____ dimes

_____ nickels

_____ pennies

C. Write your own price.

_____ half-dollars

_____ quarters

_____ dimes

_____ nickels

_____ pennies

Making Exact Amounts of Money

Pay for each item. Show what coins you use.

A.

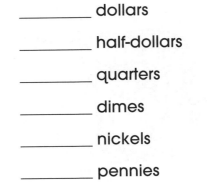

$1.30

_____ dollars

_____ half-dollars

_____ quarters

_____ dimes

_____ nickels

_____ pennies

B.

$1.55

_____ dollars

_____ half-dollars

_____ quarters

_____ dimes

_____ nickels

_____ pennies

C. Write your own price.

_____ dollars

_____ half-dollars

_____ quarters

_____ dimes

_____ nickels

_____ pennies

Pay for each treat. Use as few coins as you can.

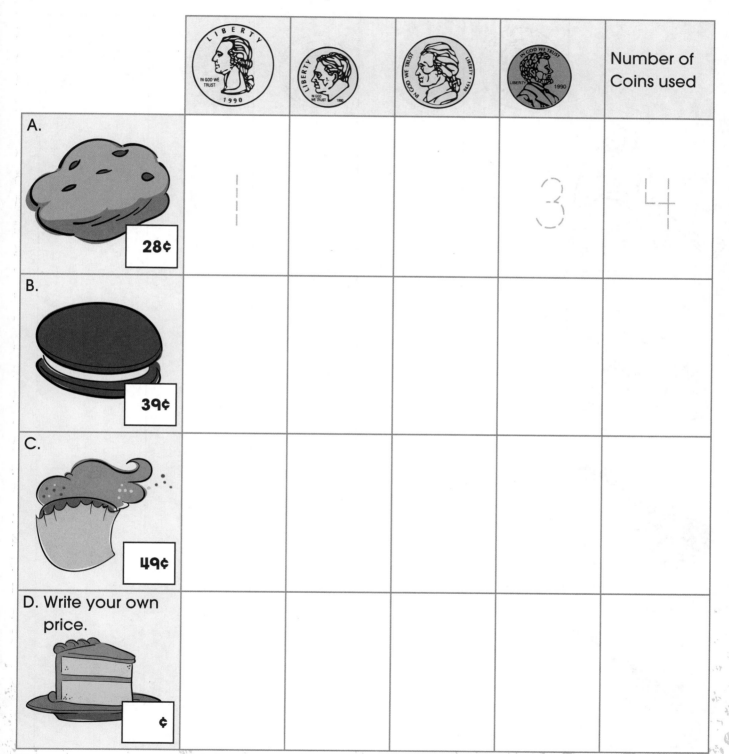

	![quarter]	![dime]	![nickel]	![penny]	Number of Coins used
A. 28¢	1			3	4
B. 39¢					
C. 49¢					
D. Write your own price. ¢					

Using Combinations of Coins to Pay

Pay for each instrument. Use as few coins as you can.

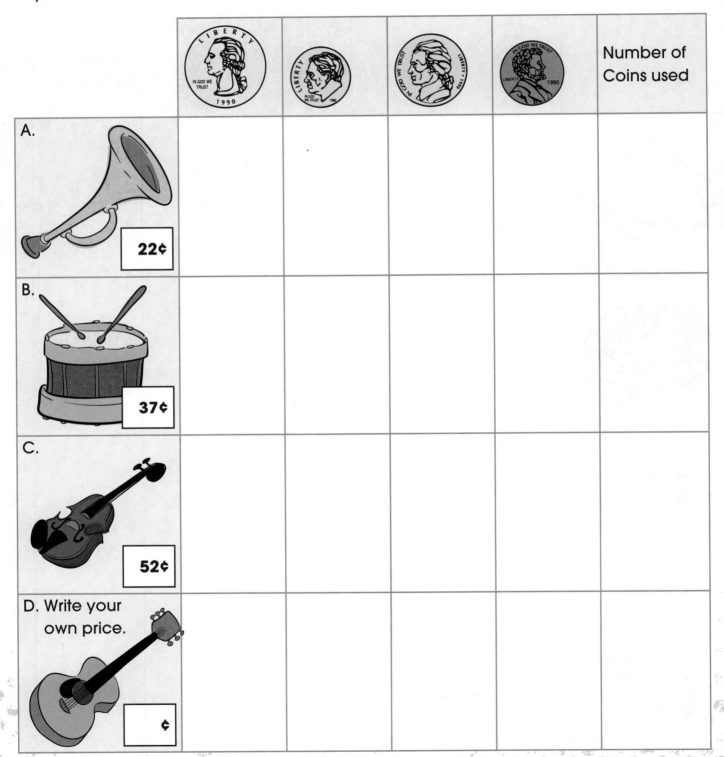

					Number of Coins used
A. 22¢					
B. 37¢					
C. 52¢					
D. Write your own price. ___¢					

Using Combinations of Coins to Pay

Pay for each book. Use as few coins as you can.

					Number of Coins used
A. SUPER 75¢					
B. SPORT 80¢					
C. Monster 97¢					
D. Write your own price. MAGIC ___¢					

Making Exact Amounts of Money Two Ways

Find two ways to pay for each item. Pay the exact amount.

A.

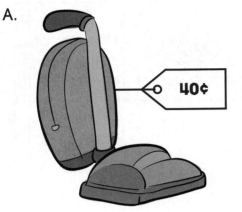

40¢

	Dimes	Nickels	Pennies
Way 1	4		
Way 2		8	

B.

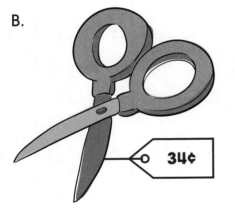

34¢

	Dimes	Nickels	Pennies
Way 1			
Way 2			

C. Write your own price.

	Dimes	Nickels	Pennies
Way 1			
Way 2			

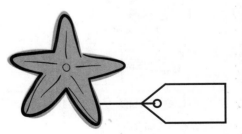

Making Exact Amounts of Money Two Ways

Find two ways to pay for each item. Pay the exact amount.

A.

52¢ MARBLE MAGNETS

	Quarters	Dimes	Nickels	Pennies
Way 1				
Way 2				

B.

75¢ STAMP PAD

	Quarters	Dimes	Nickels	Pennies
Way 1				
Way 2				

C. Write your own price.

	Quarters	Dimes	Nickels	Pennies
Way 1				
Way 2				

MONEY MYSTERIES ¢ ¢ ¢ ¢ ?????

Making Exact Amounts of Money Two Ways

Find two ways to pay for each item. Pay the exact amount.

A.

	Half-Dollars	Quarters	Dimes	Nickels	Pennies
Way 1					
Way 2					

B. $1.50

	Half-Dollars	Quarters	Dimes	Nickels	Pennies
Way 1					
Way 2					

C. Write your own price.

	Half-Dollars	Quarters	Dimes	Nickels	Pennies
Way 1					
Way 2					

Making Exact Amounts of Money Two Ways

Find two ways to pay for each item. Pay the exact amount.

$5.60

A.

	$1 Bills	Half-Dollars	Quarters	Dimes	Nickels	Pennies
Way 1						
Way 2						

$5.95

B.

	$1 Bills	Half-Dollars	Quarters	Dimes	Nickels	Pennies
Way 1						
Way 2						

C.

$6.72

Solve this puzzle.
What's missing in each way?

	$1 Bills	Half-Dollars	Quarters	Dimes	Nickels	Pennies
Way 1	6	1				12
Way 2	4		1			7

Estimating Amounts of Money

banana	pudding	popcorn	cookies	crackers & peanut butter
10¢	25¢	30¢	20¢	15¢

Use the coins shown. If you spend all your money, which snacks can you buy? First estimate. Then, check.

A.

I think I can buy: _____

I can buy: _____

B.

I think I can buy: _____

I can buy: _____

C. Solve this puzzle:

Ahmed had 1 quarter, 1 dime, 1 nickel and 10 pennies. He bought two snacks. He has less than 10 cents left. What snacks did he buy? _____

Estimating Amounts of Money

25¢	65¢	50¢	55¢	75¢	35¢

Use the coins shown. If you spend all your money, which pet treats can you buy? First estimate. Then, check.

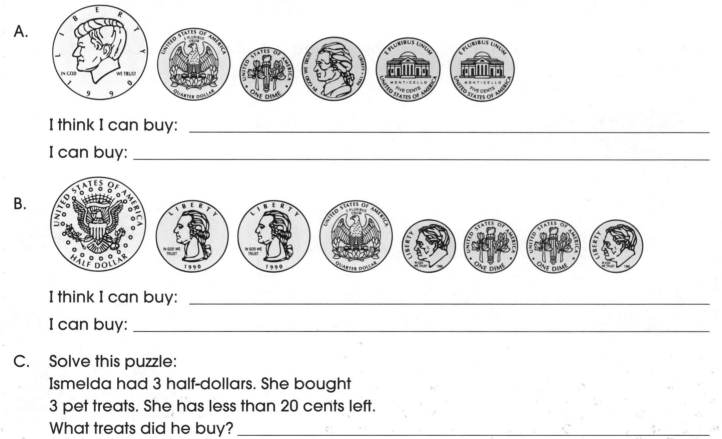

A.

I think I can buy: _____

I can buy: _____

B.

I think I can buy: _____

I can buy: _____

C. Solve this puzzle:
Ismelda had 3 half-dollars. She bought
3 pet treats. She has less than 20 cents left.
What treats did he buy? _____

Name _____

Estimating Amounts of Money

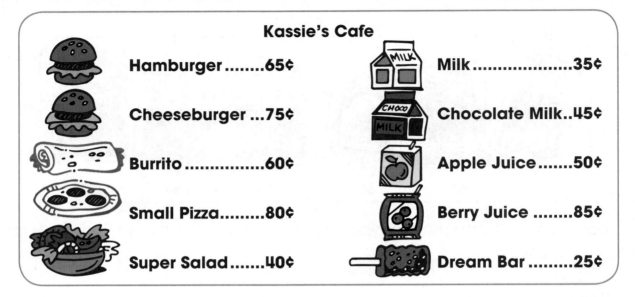

Kassie's Cafe

Hamburger ....65¢

Cheeseburger ...75¢

Burrito ....60¢

Small Pizza.........80¢

Super Salad.......40¢

Milk ....35¢

Chocolate Milk..45¢

Apple Juice.......50¢

Berry Juice ....85¢

Dream Bar ....25¢

Use the coins and bills shown. If you spend all your money, what can you buy? First estimate. Then, check.

A.

I think I can buy: _____

I can buy: _____

B.

I think I can buy: _____

I can buy: _____

C. Solve this puzzle.

Tina had 1 one-dollar bill, 1 half-dollar and 2 quarters. She bought three things. She has less than 25 cents left. What did Tina buy? _____

_____

Paying Exact Amounts and Change

Pay the exact amount. What change do you get back?

A.

Amount you get back:

_____ ¢

B.

Amount you get back:

_____ ¢

C.

Amount you get back:

_____ ¢

Paying Exact Amounts and Change

Pay the exact amount. What change do you get back?

A.

Amount you get back:

_____ ¢

B.

Amount you get back:

_____ ¢

C.

Choose a price between $1.15 and $1.28. Write the price.

Amount you get back:

_____ ¢

Paying Exact Amounts and Change

Pay the exact amount. What change do you get back?

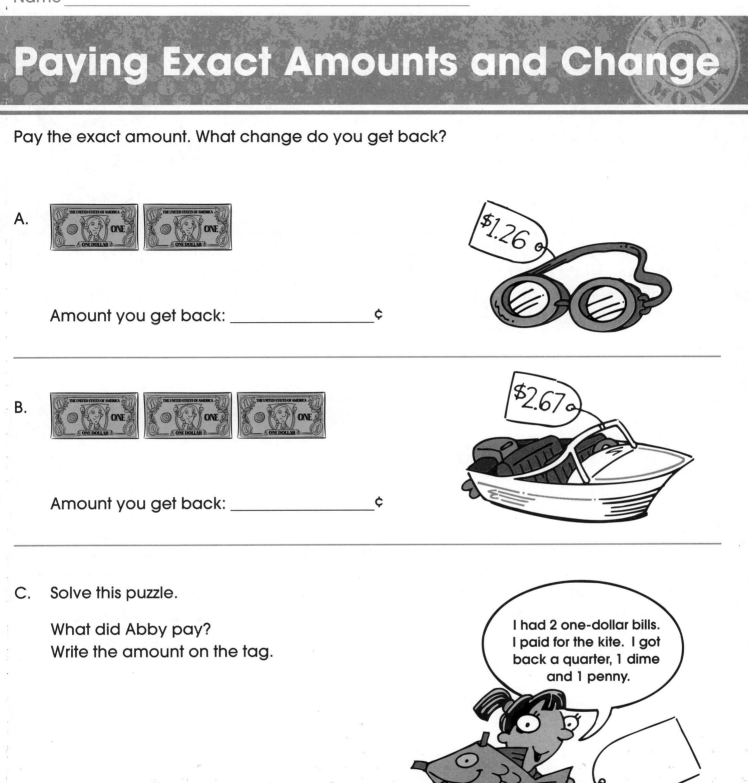

A.

Amount you get back: _____ ¢

B.

Amount you get back: _____ ¢

C. Solve this puzzle.

What did Abby pay?
Write the amount on the tag.

I had 2 one-dollar bills.
I paid for the kite. I got
back a quarter, 1 dime
and 1 penny.

Money Puzzles

Solve the puzzles. Draw the coins.

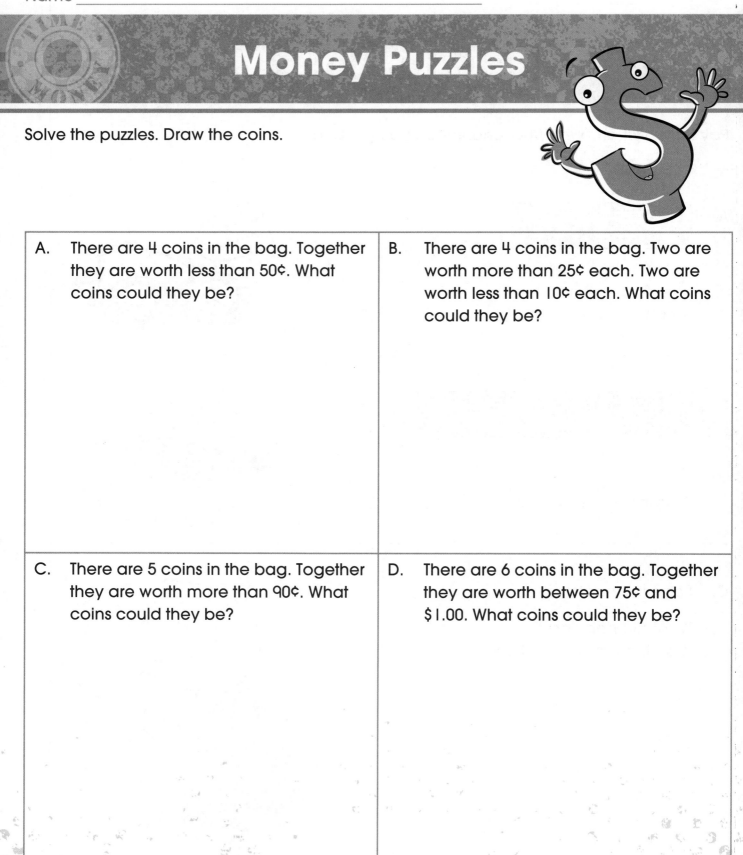

A. There are 4 coins in the bag. Together they are worth less than 50¢. What coins could they be?	**B.** There are 4 coins in the bag. Two are worth more than 25¢ each. Two are worth less than 10¢ each. What coins could they be?
C. There are 5 coins in the bag. Together they are worth more than 90¢. What coins could they be?	**D.** There are 6 coins in the bag. Together they are worth between 75¢ and $1.00. What coins could they be?

Money Puzzles

Solve the puzzles. Draw the coins.

A. There are 5 coins in the bank. Together they are worth $1.00 exactly. What coins could they be?	B. There are 6 coins in the bank. Together they are worth between 80¢ and $1.20. What coins could they be?
C. There are 6 coins in the bank. Two are worth more than 10¢ each. Four are worth less than 10¢ each. All together they are worth more than $1.00. What coins could they be?	D. There are 6 coins in the bank. Four are worth more than 10¢ each. Two are worth less than 25¢ each. All together they are worth less than $1.50. What coins could they be?

Using Combinations of Coins to Pay

Use the coins shown to make each amount..

A. Use 3 of the coins to make 25¢. What coins did you use?			2	1	
B. Use 4 of the coins to make 50¢. What coins did you use?					
C. Use 4 of the coins to make 66¢. What coins did you use?					
D. Use 5 of the coins to make 96¢. What coins did you use?					

Use the coins shown to make each amount..

	Half Dollar	Quarter	Dime	Nickel
A. Use 3 of the coins to make 60¢. What coins did you use?				
B. What other way can you do it?				
C. Use 4 of the coins to make 40¢. What coins did you use?				
D. What other way can you do it?				
E. Use 4 of the coins to make 80¢. What coins did you use?				
F. What other way can you do it?				

Name _____

Solve the money story puzzles.

A. Sean sees a box of magnets
    on sale for 50 cents. He takes
    10 coins out of his pocket and
    buys the magnets.

    What coins could they be?

B. Tyesha sees a small bag of jacks
    for 58 cents. She takes 9 coins
    out if her pocket to pay.

    What coins could they be?

C. Dustin sees a toy hammer. He
    wants to buy it for his little brother.
    He pulls six coins out of his pocket
    and pays 75 cents.

    What coins could they be?

Money Story Puzzles

Solve the money story puzzles.

A. Matt buys a box of things for doing magic tricks. He takes an even number of coins out of his pocket and pays 65 cents.

What coins could they be?

B. Stacey buys a poster for 70 cents. She uses an odd number of coins to buy it.

What coins could they be?

C. Write a money story puzzle about buying this stuffed whale.

Money Story Puzzles

Solve the money story puzzles.

A.   Amber put coins into her bank for a long time. She saved $6.25 in all. Amber saved $3.55 more than her sister Holly.

How much did Holly save?

B.   Collin and Jason each bought a watch. Jason paid $4.99 for his Flip-up Crocodile Watch. That was $1.20 more than Collin paid for his Dinosaur Watch.

How much did Collin pay?

C.   Write a money story puzzle about yourself and a friend.

Money Story Puzzles

Solve the money story puzzles.

A. Pilar and Kara fed the horses
    at the fair. Kara's mother gave
    the girls 3 one-dollar bills,
    3 quarters, 5 dimes and
    3 nickels. Darci and Kara
    divided the money equally.

    How much money did each of them get?

B. Juan and Ben washed cars one
    Saturday. When they finished,
    they had 3 one-dollar bills,
    I half dollar, three quarters,
    2 dimes and I nickel in their
    money box. The boys divided
    the money fairly.

    How much money did each of them get?

C. Write a money story puzzle about
    earning money and dividing it equally.

Money Story Puzzles

Solve the money story puzzles.

A. Eric and Alicia took all the coins out of their pockets. They put the coins together and paid 65 cents for a bag of corn chips. Alicia paid 15 cents more than Eric.

How much did each of them pay?

B. Two friends put their money together and bought a package of stickers for $1.60. Rachel paid 20 cents more than Amanda.

How much money did each girl pay?

C. Write a money story puzzle about buying something with a friend.

Answer Key

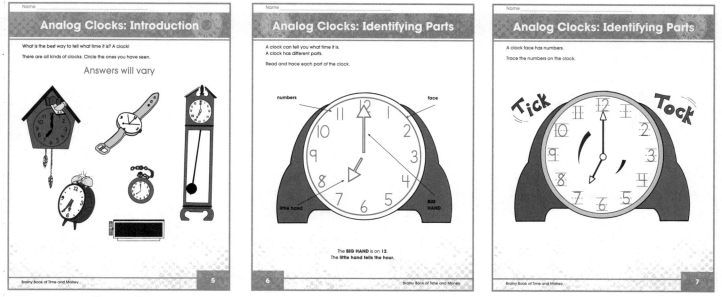

Page 5

Page 6

Page 7

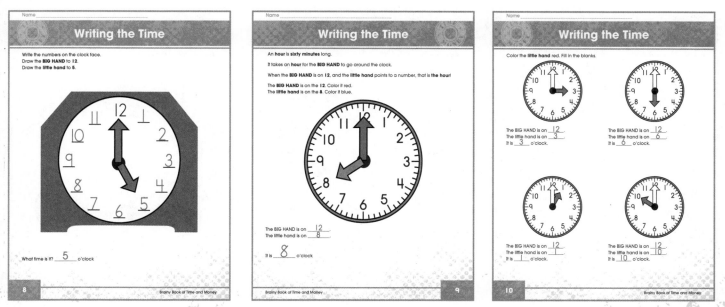

Page 8

Page 9

Page 10

Answer Key

Page 11

Page 12

Page 13

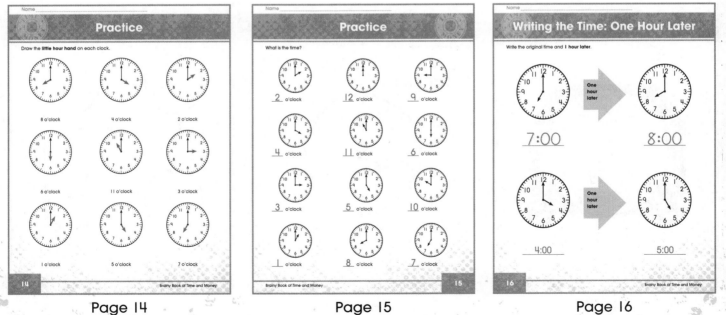

Page 14

Page 15

Page 16

Answer Key

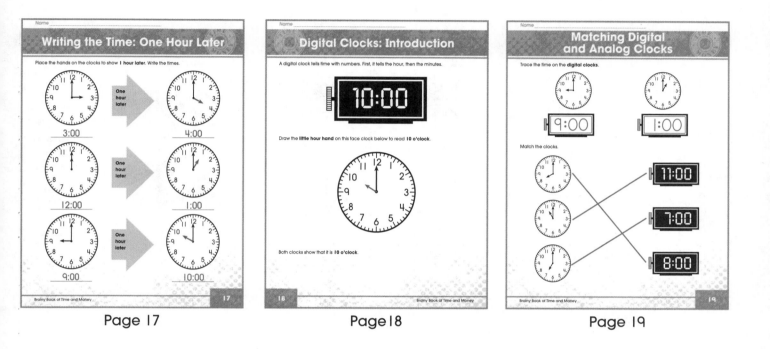

Page 17

Page 18

Page 19

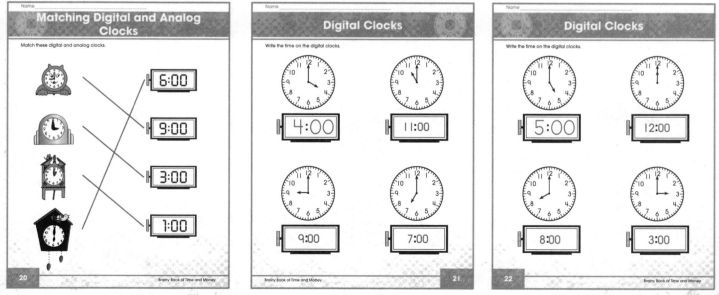

Page 20

Page 21

Page 22

Answer Key

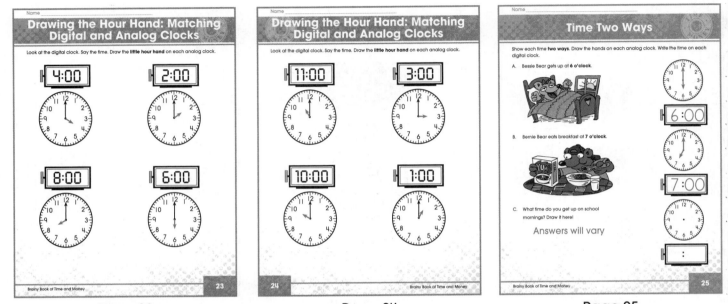

Page 23

Page 24

Page 25

Page 26

Page 27

Page 28

Answer Key

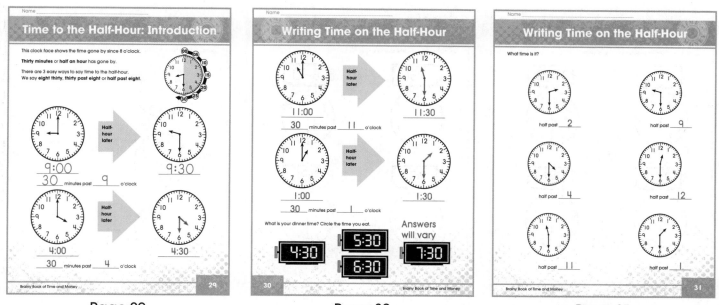

Page 29

Page 30

Page 31

Page 32

Page 33

Page 34

Answer Key

Page 35

Page 36

Page 37

Page 38

Page 39

Page 40

Answer Key

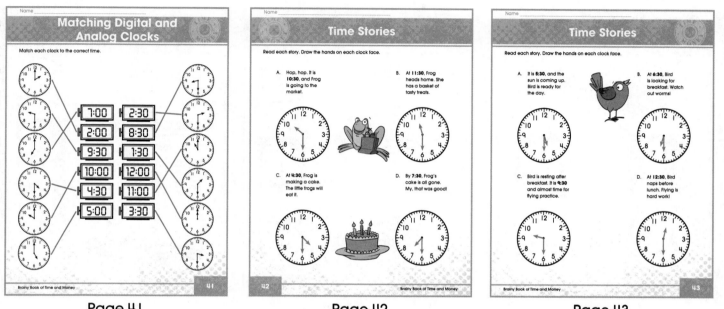

Page 41

Page 42

Page 43

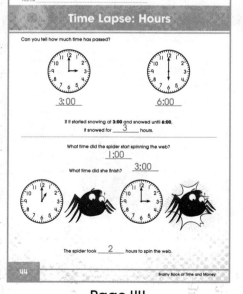

Page 44

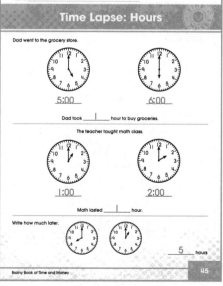

Page 45

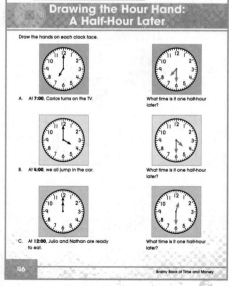

Page 46

Answer Key

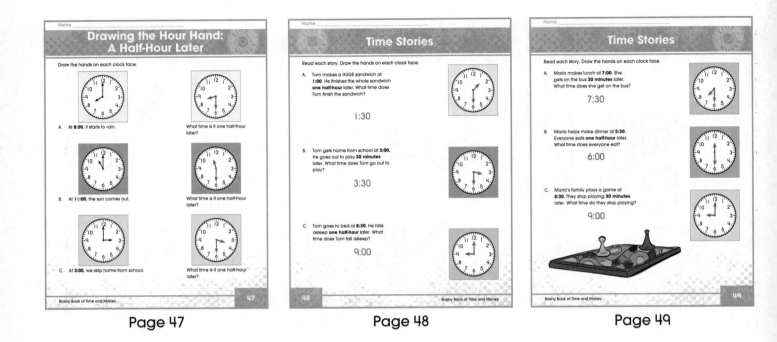

Page 47

Page 48

Page 49

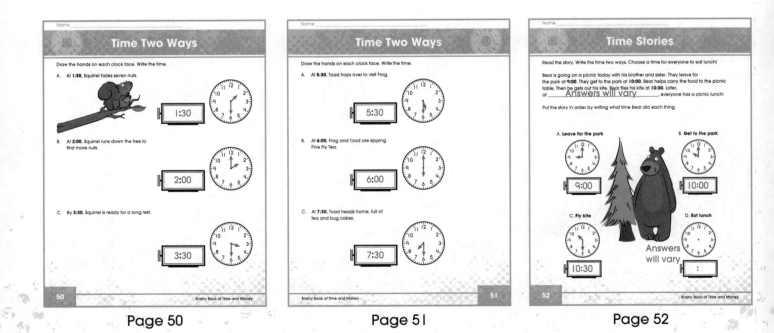

Page 50

Page 51

Page 52

Answer Key

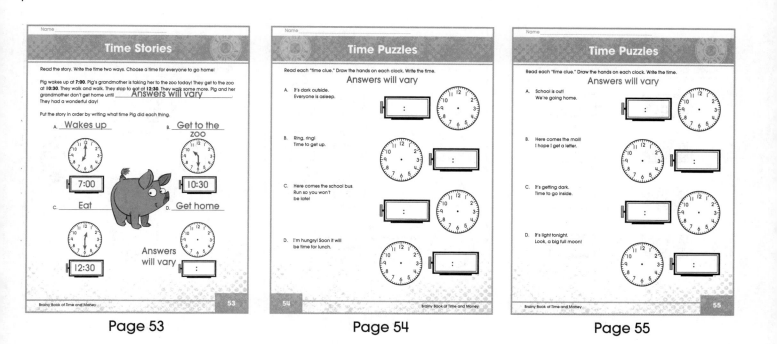

Page 53

Page 54

Page 55

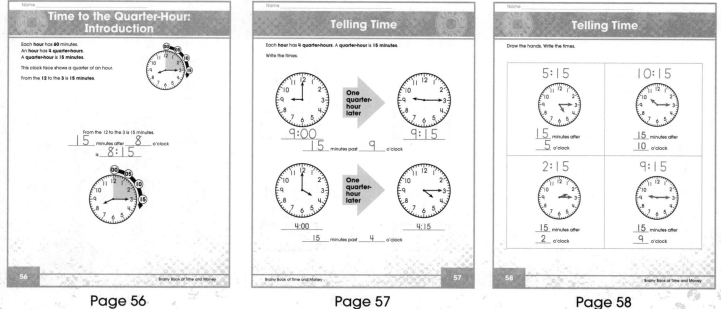

Page 56

Page 57

Page 58

Answer Key

Page 60

Digital Clocks

Circle the correct digital time.

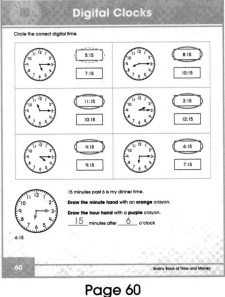

15 minutes past 6 is my dinner time.
Draw the minute hand with an **orange** crayon.
Draw the hour hand with a **purple** crayon.
__15__ minutes after __6__ o'clock

6:15

Page 61

Telling Time

Count the numbers by fives to see how many minutes have passed.

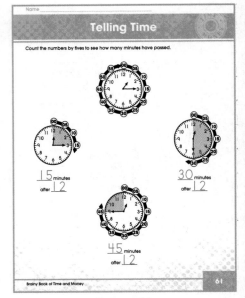

__15__ minutes after __12__

__30__ minutes after __12__

__45__ minutes after __12__

Page 62

Telling Time

Can you speak "**clock time**"?

1. "**Quarter after**" means 15 minutes after the hour.
2. "**Half past**" means 30 minutes after the hour.
3. "**Quarter to**" means 15 minutes until the next hour.

Write the quarter-hours from this time.

__8__ o'clock

quarter past __8__

half past __8__

quarter to __8__

next hour: __9__ o'clock

Page 63

Telling Time

Write the time on the digital clocks.

6:00

6:15

6:30

6:45

Page 64

Telling Time

Circle the time.

5:15	11:30
7:15	9:30
10:45	9:45
12:45	3:45
7:30	10:00
6:45	2:00
6:15	10:30
6:45	10:45
4:45	This pie bakes until a **quarter past 4.**
4:15	

230

Brainy Book of Time and Money

Answer Key

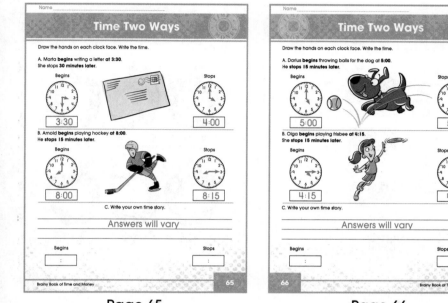

Page 65

Page 66

Page 67

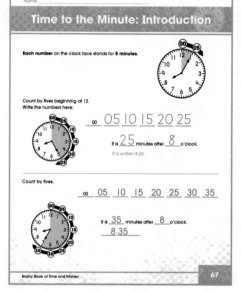

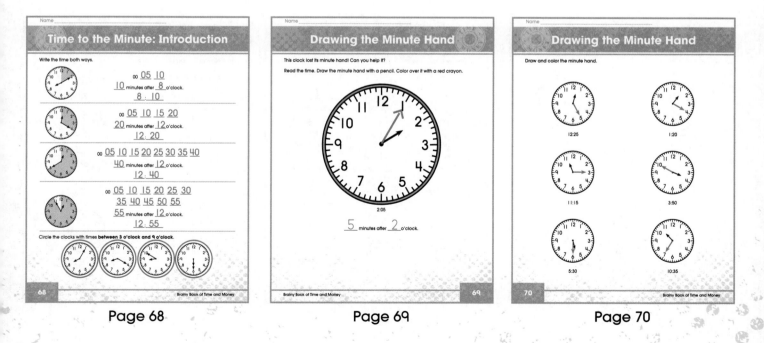

Page 68

Page 69

Page 70

Answer Key

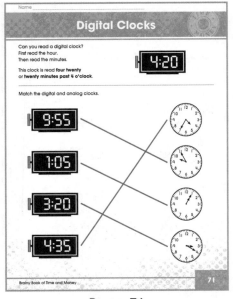

Page 71

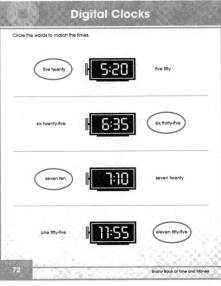

Page 72

Page 73

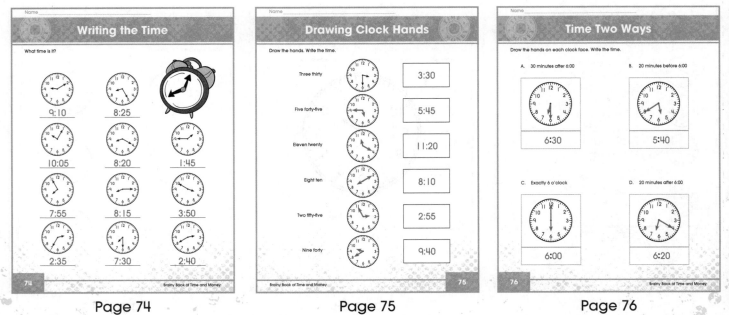

Page 74

Page 75

Page 76

Answer Key

Page 77

Page 78

Page 79

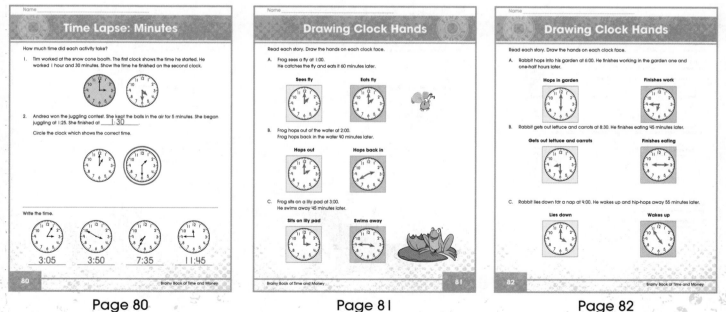

Page 80

Page 81

Page 82

Answer Key

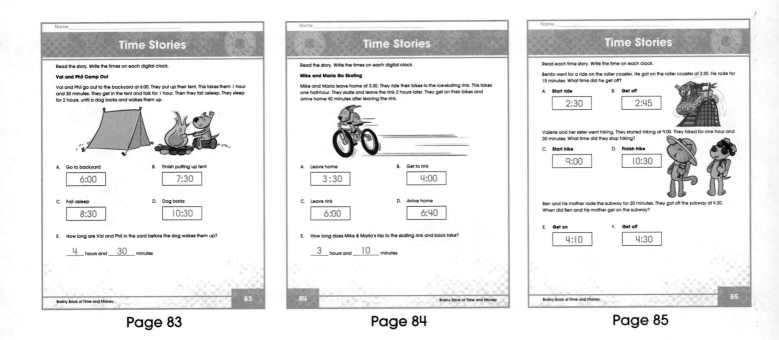

Time Stories

Read the story. Write the times on each digital clock.

Val and Phil Camp Out

Val and Phil go out to the backyard at 6:00. They put up their tent. This takes them 1 hour and 30 minutes. They get in the tent and talk for 1 hour. Then they fall asleep. They sleep for 2 hours, until a dog barks and wakes them up.

A. Go to backyard **6:00**
B. Finish putting up tent **7:30**
C. Fall asleep **8:30**
D. Dog barks **10:30**

E. How long are Val and Phil in the yard before the dog wakes them up?

4 hours and **30** minutes

Page 83

Time Stories

Read the story. Write the times on each digital clock.

Mike and Maria Go Skating

Mike and Maria leave home at 3:30. They ride their bikes to the ice-skating rink. This takes one half-hour. They skate and leave the rink 2 hours later. They get on their bikes and arrive home 40 minutes after leaving the rink.

A. Leave home **3:30**
B. Get to rink **4:00**
C. Leave rink **6:00**
D. Arrive home **6:40**

E. How long does Mike & Maria's trip to the skating rink and back take?

3 hours and **10** minutes

Page 84

Time Stories

Read each time story. Write the time on each clock.

Benito went for a ride on the roller coaster. He got on the roller coaster at 2:30. He rode for 15 minutes. What time did he get off?

A. Start ride **2:30**
B. Get off **2:45**

Valerie and her sister went hiking. They started hiking at 9:00. They hiked for one hour and 30 minutes. What time did they stop hiking?

C. Start hike **9:00**
D. Finish hike **10:30**

Ben and his mother rode the subway for 20 minutes. They got off the subway at 4:30. When did Ben and his mother get on the subway?

E. Get on **4:10**
F. Get off **4:30**

Page 85

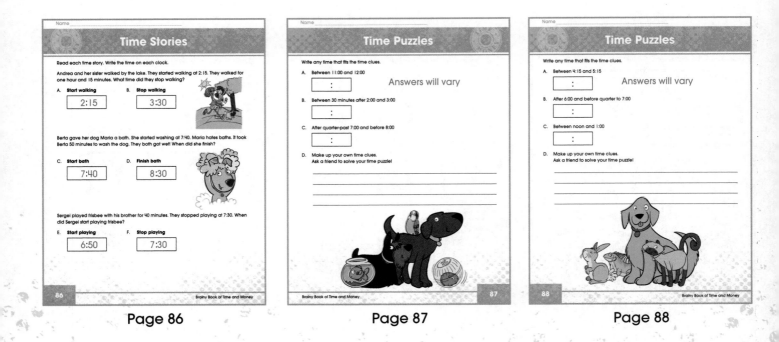

Time Stories

Read each time story. Write the time on each clock.

Andrea and her sister walked by the lake. They started walking at 2:15. They walked for one hour and 15 minutes. What time did they stop walking?

A. Start walking **2:15**
B. Stop walking **3:30**

Berta gave her dog Maria a bath. She started washing at 7:40. Maria hates baths. It took Berta 50 minutes to wash the dog. They both got wet! When did she finish?

C. Start bath **7:40**
D. Finish bath **8:30**

Sergei played frisbee with his brother for 40 minutes. They stopped playing at 7:30. When did Sergei start playing frisbee?

E. Start playing **6:50**
F. Stop playing **7:30**

Page 86

Time Puzzles

Write any time that fits the time clues.

A. Between 11:00 and 12:00 _ : _   Answers will vary

B. Between 30 minutes after 2:00 and 3:00 _ : _

C. After quarter-past 7:00 and before 8:00 _ : _

D. Make up your own time clues. Ask a friend to solve your time puzzle!

Page 87

Time Puzzles

Write any time that fits the time clues.

A. Between 4:15 and 5:15 _ : _   Answers will vary

B. After 6:00 and before quarter to 7:00 _ : _

C. Between noon and 1:00 _ : _

D. Make up your own time clues. Ask a friend to solve your time puzzle!

Page 88

Answer Key

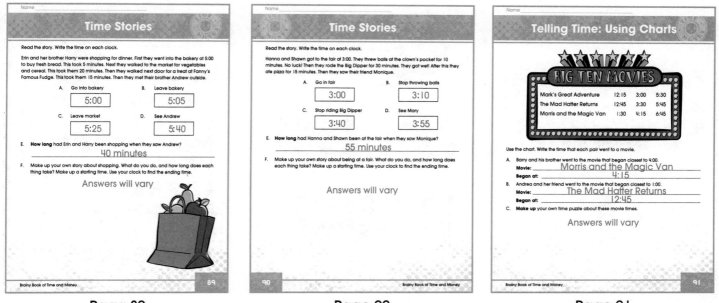

Page 89

Time Stories

Read the story. Write the time on each clock.

Erin and her brother Harry were shopping for dinner. First they went into the bakery at 5:00 to buy fresh bread. This took 5 minutes. Next they walked to the market for vegetables and cereal. This took them 20 minutes. Then they walked next door for a treat at Fanny's Famous Fudge. This took them 15 minutes. Then they met their brother Andrew outside.

A. Go into bakery — **5:00**   B. Leave bakery — **5:05**
C. Leave market — **5:25**   D. See Andrew — **5:40**

E. **How long** had Erin and Harry been shopping when they saw Andrew?
40 minutes

F. Make up your own story about shopping. What do you do, and how long does each thing take? Make up your clock to find the ending time.

Answers will vary

Page 90

Time Stories

Read the story. Write the time on each clock.

Hanna and Shawn got to the fair at 3:00. They threw balls at the clown's pocket for 10 minutes. No luck! Then they rode the Big Dipper for 30 minutes. They got wet! After this they ate pizza for 15 minutes. Then they saw their friend Monique.

A. Go in fair — **3:00**   B. Stop throwing balls — **3:10**
C. Stop riding Big Dipper — **3:40**   D. See Mary — **3:55**

E. **How long** had Hanna and Shawn been at the fair when they saw Monique?
55 minutes

F. Make up your own story about being at a fair. What do you do, and how long does each thing take? Make up a starting time. Use your clock to find the ending time.

Answers will vary

Page 91

Telling Time: Using Charts

BIG TEN MOVIES

Mark's Great Adventure	12:15	3:00	5:30
The Mad Hatter Returns	12:45	3:30	5:45
Morris and the Magic Van	1:30	4:15	6:45

Use the chart. Write the time that each pair went to a movie.

A. Barry and his brother went to the movie that began closest to 4:00.
Movie: **Morris and the Magic Van**
Began at: **4:15**

B. Andrea and her friend went to the movie that began closest to 1:00.
Movie: **The Mad Hatter Returns**
Began at: **12:45**

C. **Make up** your own time puzzle about these movie times.

Answers will vary

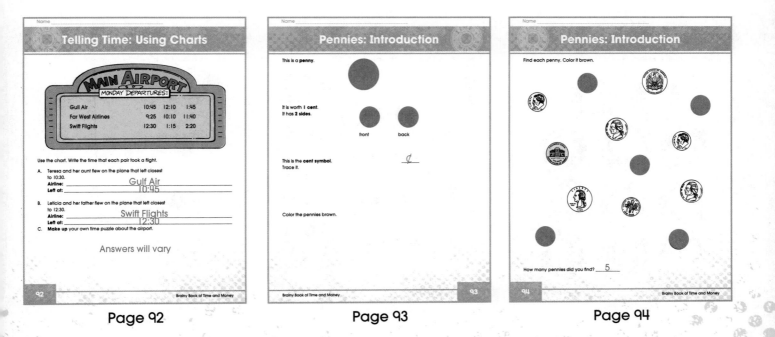

Page 92

Telling Time: Using Charts

MAIN AIRPORT
MONDAY DEPARTURES:

Gull Air	10:45	12:10	1:45
Far West Airlines	9:25	10:10	11:40
Swift Flights	12:30	1:15	2:20

Use the chart. Write the time that each pair took a flight.

A. Teresa and her aunt flew on the plane that left closest to 10:30.
Airline: **Gulf Air**
Left at: **10:45**

B. Leticia and her father flew on the plane that left closest to 12:30.
Airline: **Swift Flights**
Left at: **12:30**

C. **Make up** your own time puzzle about the airport.

Answers will vary

Page 93

Pennies: Introduction

This is a **penny**.

It is worth **1 cent**.
It has **2 sides**.

front   back

This is the **cent symbol**.
Trace it.

Color the pennies brown.

Page 94

Pennies: Introduction

Find each penny. Color it brown.

How many pennies did you find? **5**

Answer Key

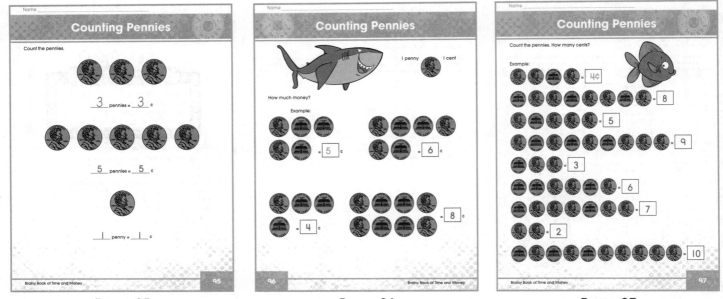

Page 95

Page 96

Page 97

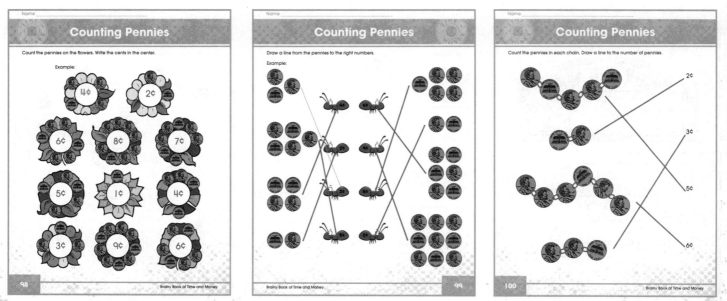

Page 98

Page 99

Page 100

Answer Key

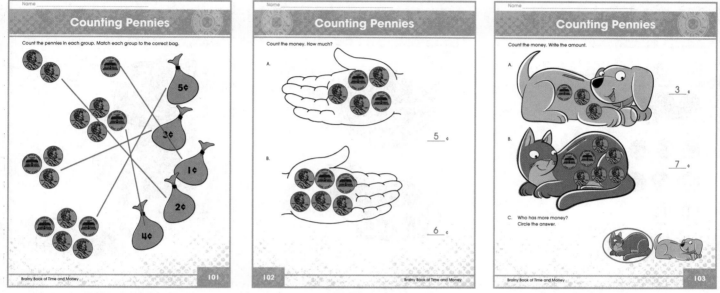

Page 101

Page 102

Page 103

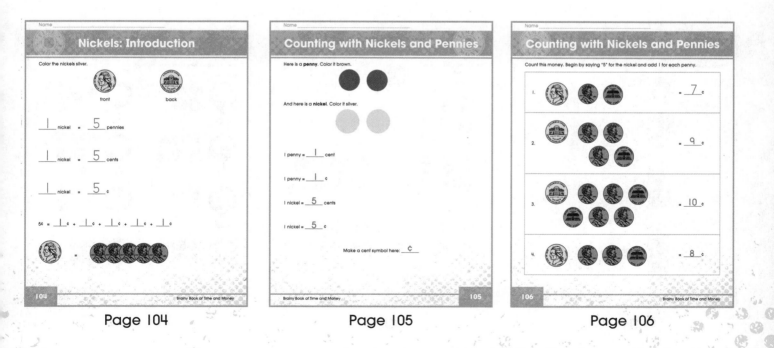

Page 104

Page 105

Page 106

Answer Key

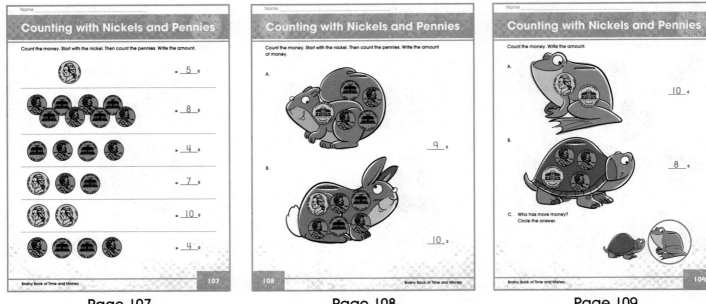

Page 107

Page 108

Page 109

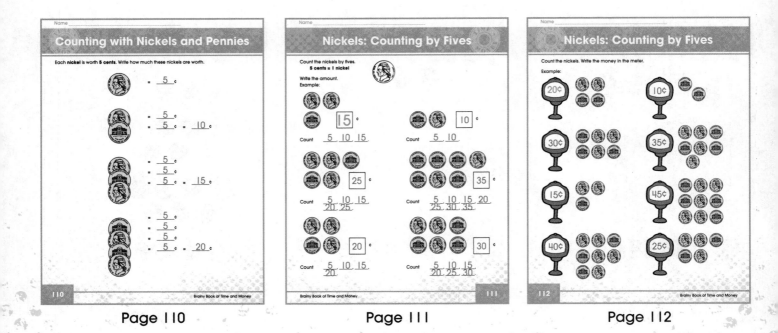

Page 110

Page 111

Page 112

Answer Key

Page 113

Page 114

Page 115

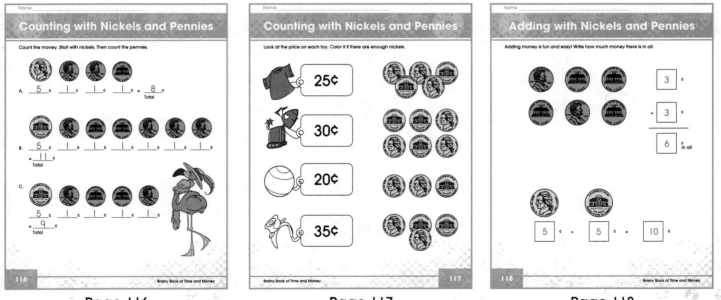

Page 116

Page 117

Page 118

Answer Key

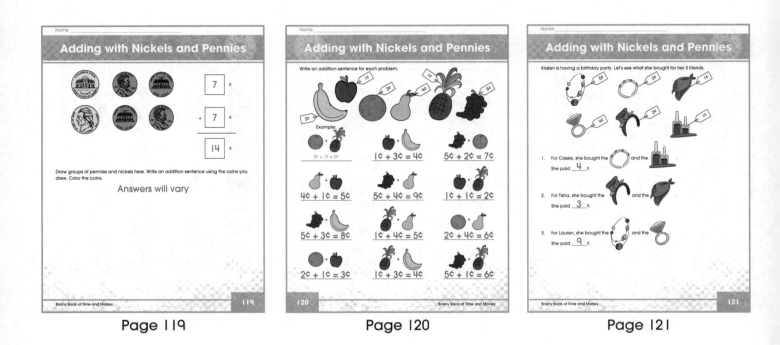

Page 119

Page 120

Page 121

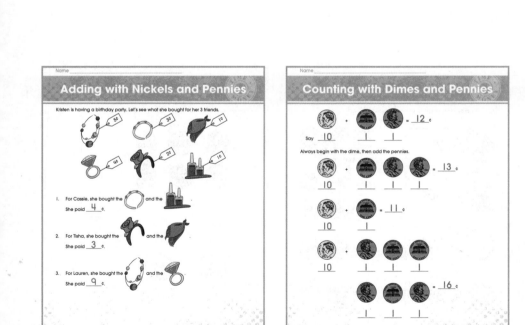

Page 122

Page 123

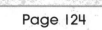

Page 124

240

Brainy Book of Time and Money

Answer Key

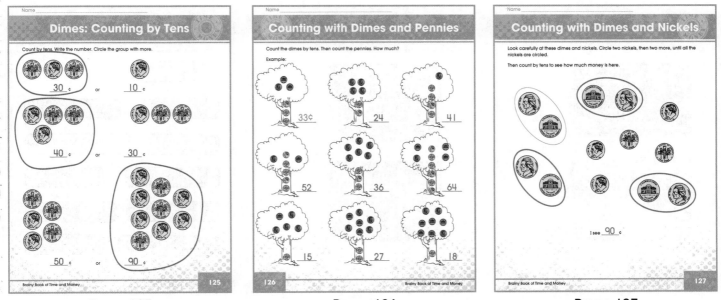

Page 125

Page 126

Page 127

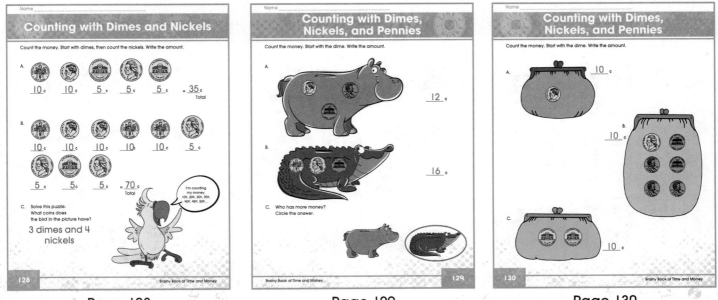

Page 128

Page 129

Page 130

Answer Key

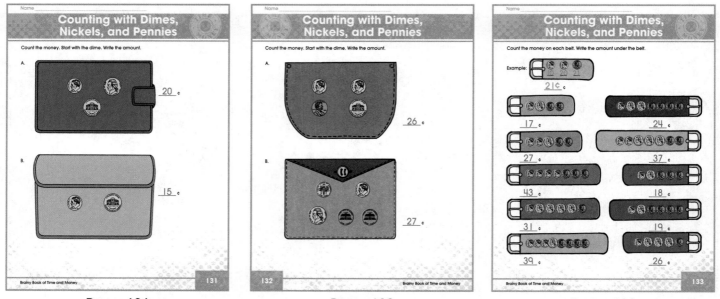

Page 131

Page 132

Page 133

Page 134

Page 135

Page 136

Answer Key

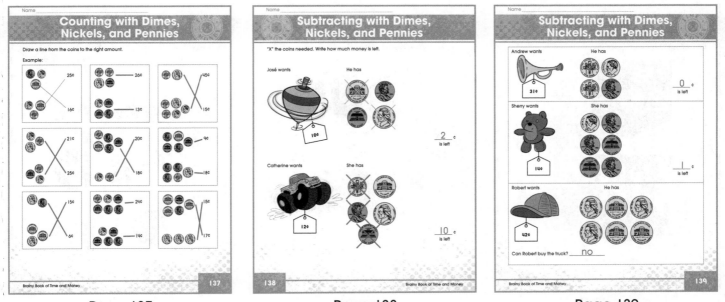

Page 137

Page 138

Page 139

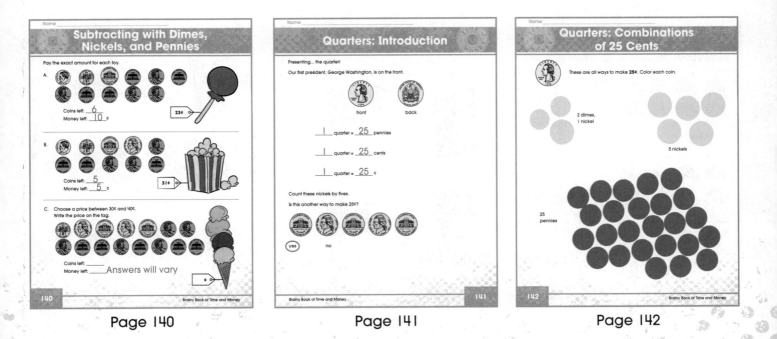

Page 140

Page 141

Page 142

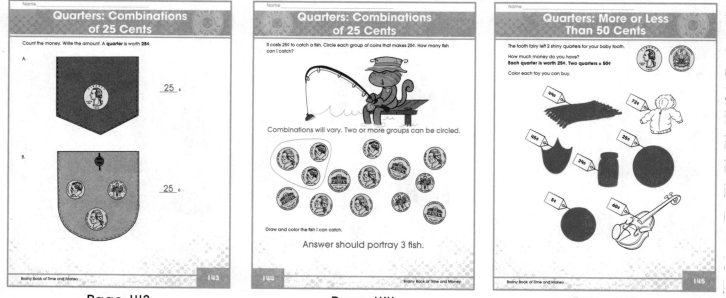

Page 143

Page 144

Page 145

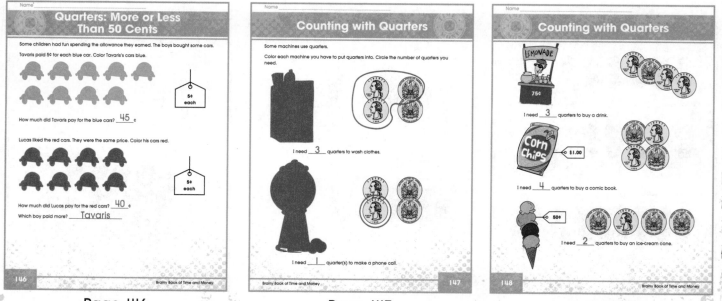

Page 146

Page 147

Page 148

Answer Key

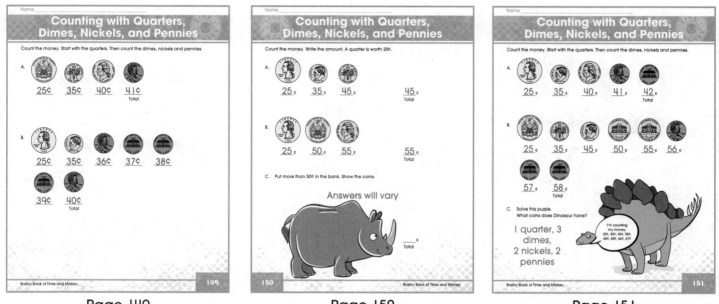

Page 149

Name_____

Counting with Quarters, Dimes, Nickels, and Pennies

Count the money. Start with the quarters. Then count the dimes, nickels and pennies.

A. 25¢ 35¢ 40¢ 41¢
Total

B. 25¢ 35¢ 36¢ 37¢ 38¢

39¢ 40¢
Total

Brainy Book of Time and Money   149

Page 150

Name_____

Counting with Quarters, Dimes, Nickels, and Pennies

Count the money. Write the amount. A quarter is worth 25¢.

A. 25¢ 35¢ 45¢   45¢
Total

B. 25¢ 50¢ 55¢   55¢
Total

C. Put more than 50¢ in the bank. Show the coins.

Answers will vary

_____ ¢
Total

150   *Brainy Book of Time and Money*

Page 151

Name_____

Counting with Quarters, Dimes, Nickels, and Pennies

Count the money. Start with the quarters. Then count the dimes, nickels and pennies.

A. 25¢ 35¢ 40¢ 41¢ 42¢
Total

B. 25¢ 35¢ 45¢ 50¢ 55¢ 56¢

57¢ 58¢
Total

C. Solve this puzzle. What coins does Dinosaur have?

1 quarter, 3 dimes, 2 nickels, 2 pennies

I'm counting my money. 25¢, 35¢, 45¢, 55¢, 60¢, 65¢, 66¢, 67¢

Brainy Book of Time and Money   151

Page 152

Name_____

Counting with Quarters, Dimes, Nickels, and Pennies

Count the money. Start with the quarter. Write the amount.

A. 36 ¢

B. 31 ¢

152   *Brainy Book of Time and Money*

Page 153

Name_____

Counting with Quarters, Dimes, Nickels, and Pennies

Match the money with the amount.

35¢
36¢
40¢
27¢
15¢
21¢
8¢

Brainy Book of Time and Money   153

Page 154

Name_____

Counting with Quarters, Dimes, Nickels, and Pennies

Count the coins. Do you have enough money to buy each toy?

	You have...	yes or no
58¢		51¢ no
47¢		57¢ yes
75¢		76¢ yes
43¢		51¢ yes
98¢		80¢ no
32¢		25¢ no
26¢		29¢ yes
45¢		35¢ no

154   *Brainy Book of Time and Money*

Answer Key

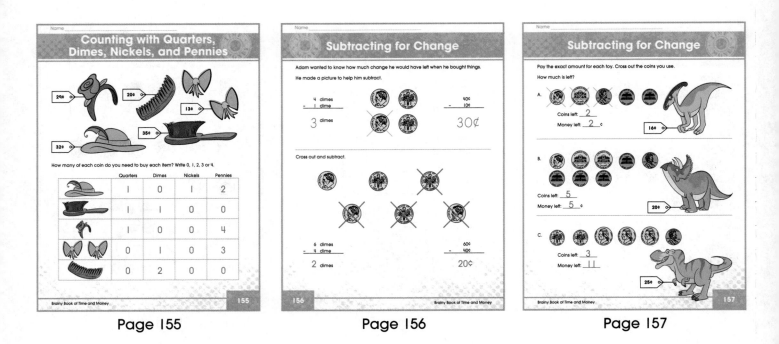

Page 155

Page 156

Page 157

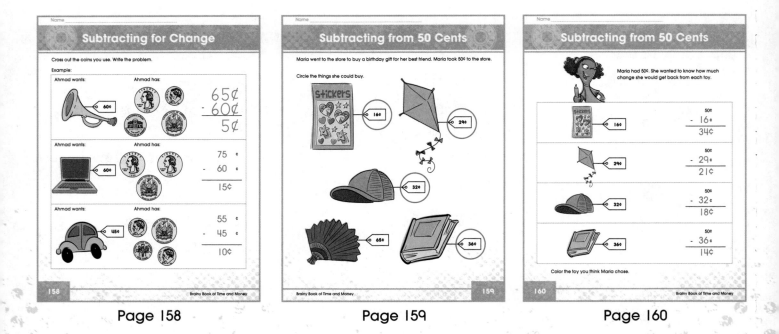

Page 158

Page 159

Page 160

Answer Key

Making Exact Amounts of Money

Use dimes, nickels and pennies. Pay the exact amount for each toy.

A. What coins did you use?

   1 dimes   0 nickels
   0 pennies

B. What coins did you use?

   1 dimes   1 nickels
   4 pennies

C. Solve this puzzle.

   What coins did Cat use to pay for the ball?

   1 dimes   1 nickels
   0 pennies

Brainy Book of Time and Money

161

Page 161

Making Exact Amounts of Money

Use dimes, nickels and pennies. Pay the exact amount for each toy.

A. What coins did you use?

   2 dimes   0 nickels
   1 pennies

   21¢

B. What coins did you use?

   1 quarters   1 dimes
   0 nickels   2 pennies

   37¢

C. Solve this puzzle.

   What coins did Alligator use to pay for the toothbrush?

   1 dimes   2 nickels
   0 pennies

   20¢

162

Brainy Book of Time and Money

Page 162

Making Exact Amounts of Money

Use quarters, dimes, nickels and pennies. Pay the exact amount for each toy.

A. What coins did you use?

   1 quarters   0 dimes
   0 nickels   2 pennies

   27¢

B. What coins did you use?

   1 quarters   1 dimes
   1 nickels   0 pennies

   40¢

C. Solve this puzzle.

   What coins did Cat use to pay for the hair bows?

   1 quarters   0 dimes
   1 nickels   0 pennies

   30¢

Brainy Book of Time and Money

163

Page 163

Making Exact Amounts of Money and Change

Use the coins shown. Pay the exact amount for each toy.
How much do you have left?

A.

   Coins left: 5
   Money left: 5 ¢

   37 ¢

B.

   Coins left: 0
   Money left: 0 ¢

   50¢

C.

   Choose a price between 42¢ and 58¢. Write the price on the tag.

   Answers will vary

   Coins left: _____
   Money left: _____ ¢

   ¢

164

Brainy Book of Time and Money

Page 164

Making Exact Amounts of Money and Change

Use the coins shown. Pay the exact amount for each toy.

A.

   Coins left: 0
   Money left: 0 ¢

   48¢

B.

   Coins left: 6
   Money left: 10 ¢

   53¢

C. Solve this puzzle.

   How much money does Turtle have left?

   Coins left: 1
   Money left: 5 ¢

   27¢

   I had 2 dimes, 2 nickels and 2 pennies. Now I have one coin left.

Brainy Book of Time and Money

165

Page 165

Problem Solving with Money

Draw the coins you use. Write the number of coins on each blank.

A.

   9¢

   5 1 1 1 1

   0 dimes
   1 nickels
   4 pennies

B.

   11¢

   10 1

   0 dimes
   1 nickels
   4 pennies

C.

   14¢

   10 1 1 1 1

   1 dimes
   0 nickels
   4 pennies

D. Find another way to pay for the cup.

   14¢

   1 1 1 1 5 5

   0 dimes
   2 nickels
   4 pennies

166

Brainy Book of Time and Money

Page 166

Answer Key

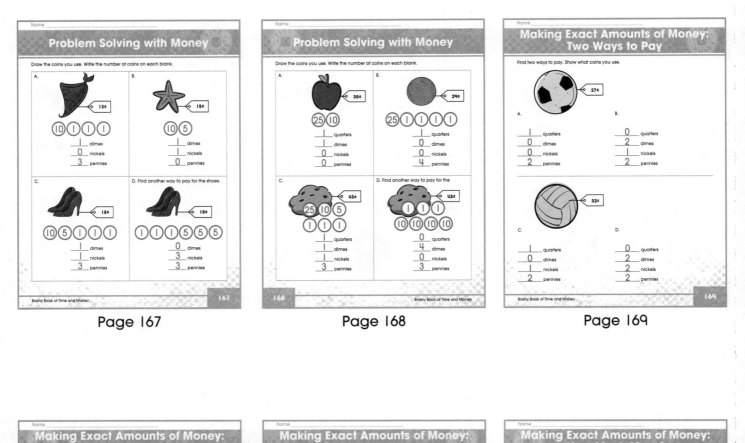

Page 167   Page 168   Page 169

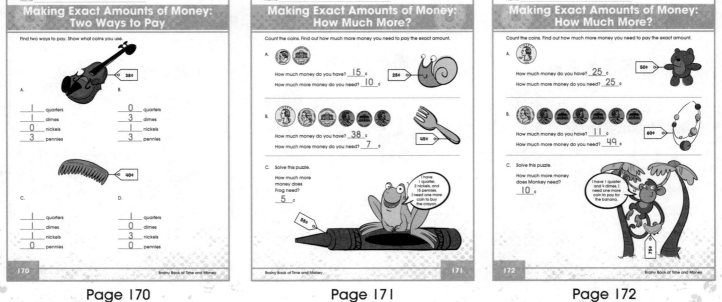

Page 170   Page 171   Page 172

Answer Key

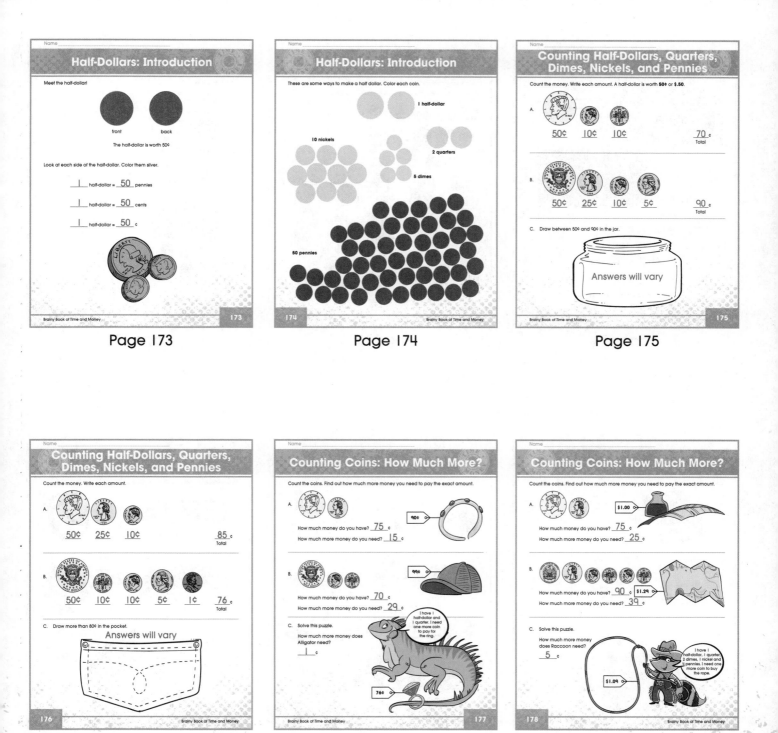

Page 173

Page 174

Page 175

Page 176

Page 177

Page 178

Answer Key

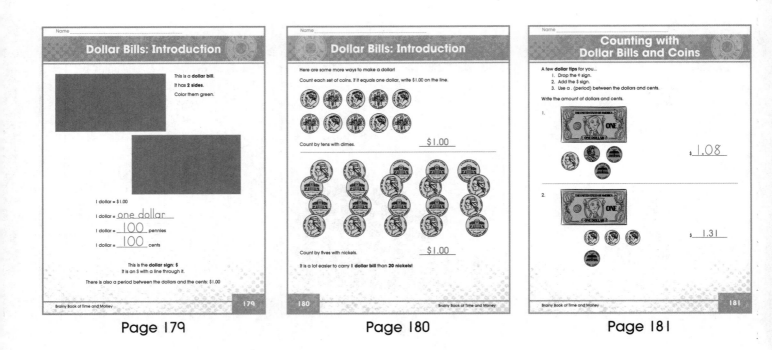

Page 179

Page 180

Page 181

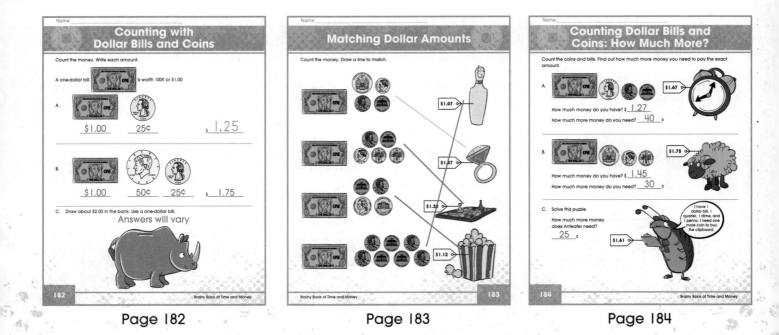

Page 182

Page 183

Page 184

Answer Key

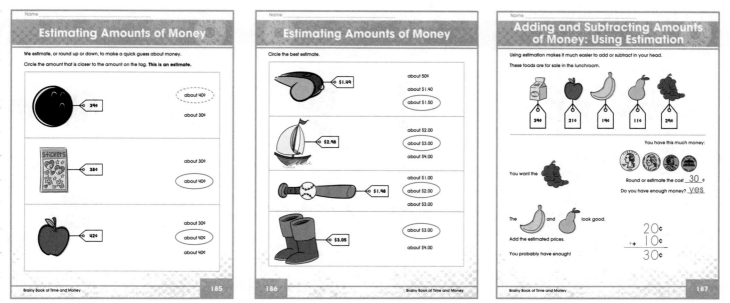

Page 185   Page 186   Page 187

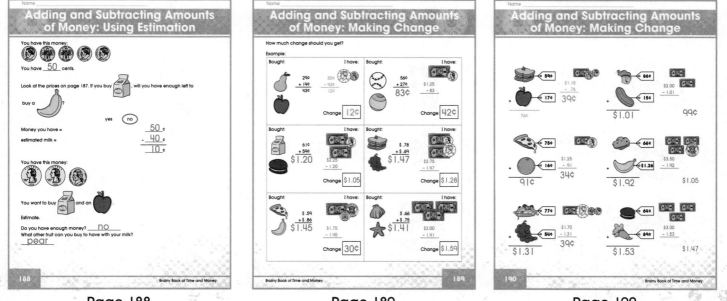

Page 188   Page 189   Page 190

Answer Key

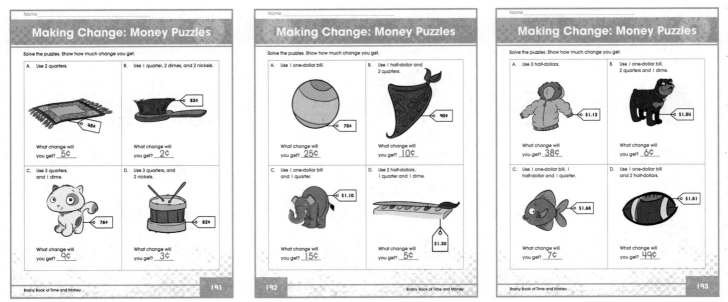

Page 191

Page 192

Page 193

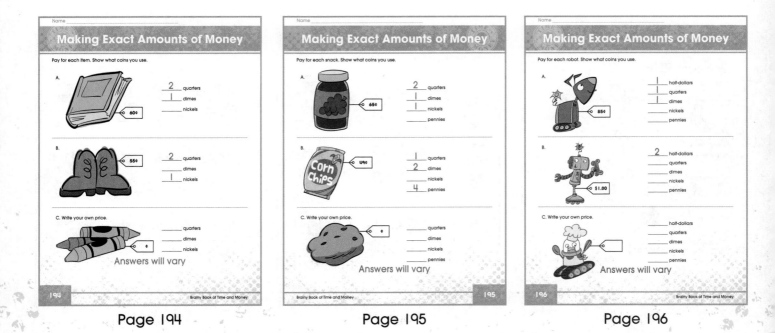

Page 194

Page 195

Page 196

Answer Key

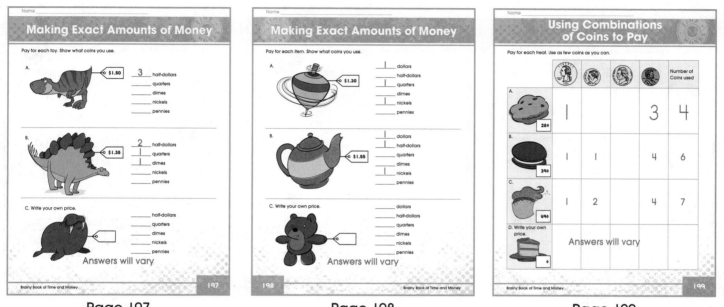

Page 197

Page 198

Page 199

Page 200

Page 201

Page 202

Answer Key

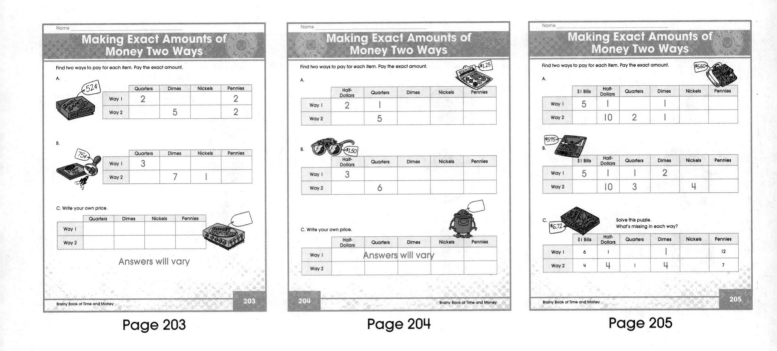

Page 203

Making Exact Amounts of Money Two Ways

Find two ways to pay for each item. Pay the exact amount.

A. 52¢

	Quarters	Dimes	Nickels	Pennies
Way 1	2			2
Way 2		5		2

B. 75¢

	Quarters	Dimes	Nickels	Pennies
Way 1	3			
Way 2		7	1	

C. Write your own price.

	Quarters	Dimes	Nickels	Pennies
Way 1				
Way 2				

Answers will vary

Page 204

Making Exact Amounts of Money Two Ways

Find two ways to pay for each item. Pay the exact amount.

A. $1.25

	Half-Dollars	Quarters	Dimes	Nickels	Pennies
Way 1	2	1			
Way 2		5			

B. $1.50

	Half-Dollars	Quarters	Dimes	Nickels	Pennies
Way 1	3				
Way 2		6			

C. Write your own price.

	Half-Dollars	Quarters	Dimes	Nickels	Pennies
Way 1			Answers will vary		
Way 2					

Page 205

Making Exact Amounts of Money Two Ways

Find two ways to pay for each item. Pay the exact amount.

A. $5.60

	$1 Bills	Half-Dollars	Quarters	Dimes	Nickels	Pennies
Way 1	5	1		1		
Way 2			10	2	1	

B. $5.95

	$1 Bills	Half-Dollars	Quarters	Dimes	Nickels	Pennies
Way 1	5	1	1	2		
Way 2			10	3		4

C. $6.72 Solve this puzzle. What's missing in each way?

	$1 Bills	Half-Dollars	Quarters	Dimes	Nickels	Pennies
Way 1	6	1		1		12
Way 2	4	4	1	4		7

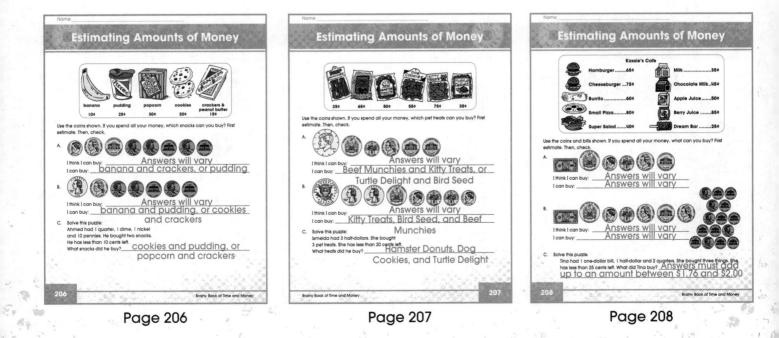

Page 206

Estimating Amounts of Money

banana 10¢ — pudding 30¢ — popcorn 20¢ — cookies 20¢ — crackers & peanut butter 15¢

Use the coins shown. If you spend all your money, which snacks can you buy? First estimate. Then, check.

A. I think I can buy: Answers will vary
I can buy: banana and crackers, or pudding

B. I think I can buy: Answers will vary
I can buy: banana and pudding, or cookies and crackers

C. Solve this puzzle:
Ahmed had 1 quarter, 1 dime, 1 nickel and 10 pennies. He bought two snacks. He has less than 10 cents left. What snacks did he buy? cookies and pudding, or popcorn and crackers

Page 207

Estimating Amounts of Money

25¢ — 65¢ — 50¢ — 55¢ — 75¢ — 35¢

Use the coins shown. If you spend all your money, which pet treats can you buy? First estimate. Then, check.

A. I think I can buy: Answers will vary
I can buy: Beef Munchies and Kitty Treats, or Turtle Delight and Bird Seed

B. I think I can buy: Answers will vary
I can buy: Kitty Treats, Bird Seed, and Beef Munchies

C. Solve this puzzle:
Ismelda had 3 half-dollars. She bought 3 pet treats. She has less than 20 cents left. What treats did he buy? Hamster Donuts, Dog Cookies, and Turtle Delight

Page 208

Estimating Amounts of Money

Kassie's Cafe

Hamburger ......65¢	Milk ....35¢
Cheeseburger ...75¢	Chocolate Milk..45¢
Burrito ....60¢	Apple Juice.......50¢
Small Pizza......80¢	Berry Juice ....85¢
Super Salad......40¢	Dream Bar ....25¢

Use the coins and bills shown. If you spend all your money, what can you buy? First estimate. Then, check.

A. I think I can buy: Answers will vary
I can buy: Answers will vary

B. I think I can buy: Answers will vary
I can buy: Answers will vary

C. Solve this puzzle.
Tina had 1 one-dollar bill, 1 half-dollar and 2 quarters. She bought three things. She has less than 25 cents left. What did Tina buy? Answers must add up to an amount between $1.76 and $2.00

Answer Key

Paying Exact Amounts and Change

Pay the exact amount. What change do you get back?

A. Amount you get back: 9 ¢

B. Amount you get back: 17 ¢

C. Amount you get back: 30 ¢

Brainy Book of Time and Money 209

Page 209

Paying Exact Amounts and Change

Pay the exact amount. What change do you get back?

A. Amount you get back: 19 ¢

B. Amount you get back: 20 ¢

C. Choose a price between $1.15 and $1.28. Write the price. Amount you get back: Answers will vary

210 Brainy Book of Time and Money

Page 210

Paying Exact Amounts and Change

Pay the exact amount. What change do you get back?

A. Amount you get back: 74 ¢

B. Amount you get back: 33 ¢

C. Solve this puzzle. What did Abby pay? Write the amount on the tag.

I had 2 one-dollar bills. I paid for the kite. I got back a quarter, 1 dime and 1 penny.

$1.64

Brainy Book of Time and Money 211

Page 211

Money Puzzles

Solve the puzzles. Draw the coins.

A. There are 4 coins in the bag. Together they are worth less than 50¢. What coins could they be?

Answers will vary

B. There are 4 coins in the bag. Two are worth more than 25¢ each. Two are worth less than 10¢ each. What coins could they be?

half-dollars, pennies, and nickels

C. There are 5 coins in the bag. Together they are worth more than 90¢. What coins could they be?

Answers will vary

D. There are 6 coins in the bag. Together they are worth between 75¢ and $1.00. What coins could they be?

Answers will vary

212 Brainy Book of Time and Money

Page 212

Money Puzzles

Solve the puzzles. Draw the coins.

A. There are 5 coins in the bank. Together they are worth $1.00 exactly. What coins could they be?

50 25 10 10 5

B. There are 6 coins in the bank. Together they are worth between 80¢ and $1.20. What coins could they be?

Answers will vary

C. There are 6 coins in the bank. Two are worth more than 10¢ each. Four are worth less than 10¢ each. All together they are worth more than $1.00. What coins could they be?

Answers will vary

D. There are 6 coins in the bank. Four are worth more than 25¢ each. Two are worth less than 25¢ each. All together they are worth less than $1.50. What coins could they be?

Answers will vary

Brainy Book of Time and Money 213

Page 213

Using Combinations of Coins to Pay

Use the coins shown to make each amount.

A. Use 3 of the coins to make 25¢. What coins did you use?			2	1
B. Use 4 of the coins to make 50¢. What coins did you use?		1	2	1
C. Use 4 of the coins to make 66¢. What coins did you use?	1		1	1
D. Use 5 of the coins to make 96¢. What coins did you use?	1	1	2	1

214 Brainy Book of Time and Money

Page 214

Answer Key

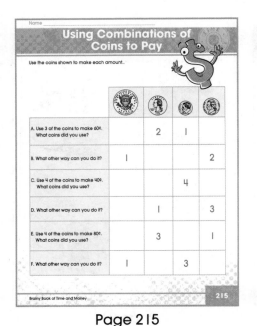

Using Combinations of Coins to Pay

Use the coins shown to make each amount..

A. Use 3 of the coins to make 60¢. What coins did you use?		2	1	
B. What other way can you do it?	1			2
C. Use 4 of the coins to make 40¢. What coins did you use?			4	
D. What other way can you do it?			1	3
E. Use 4 of the coins to make 80¢. What coins did you use?		3		1
F. What other way can you do it?	1		3	

Brainy Book of Time and Money
215

Page 215

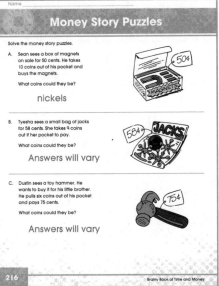

Money Story Puzzles

Solve the money story puzzles.

A. Sean sees a box of magnets on sale for 50 cents. He takes 10 coins out of his pocket and buys the magnets.

What coins could they be?

nickels

B. Tyesha sees a small bag of jacks for 58 cents. She takes 9 coins out if her pocket to pay.

What coins could they be?

Answers will vary

C. Dustin sees a toy hammer. He wants to buy it for his little brother. He pulls six coins out of his pocket and pays 75 cents.

What coins could they be?

Answers will vary

216   Brainy Book of Time and Money

Page 216

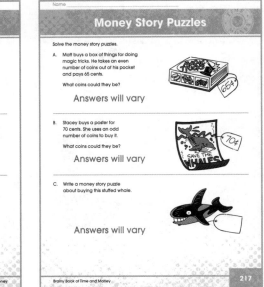

Money Story Puzzles

Solve the money story puzzles.

A. Matt buys a box of things for doing magic tricks. He takes an even number of coins out of his pocket and pays 65 cents.

What coins could they be?

Answers will vary

B. Stacey buys a poster for 70 cents. She uses an odd number of coins to buy it.

What coins could they be?

Answers will vary

C. Write a money story puzzle about buying this stuffed whale.

Answers will vary

Brainy Book of Time and Money   217

Page 217

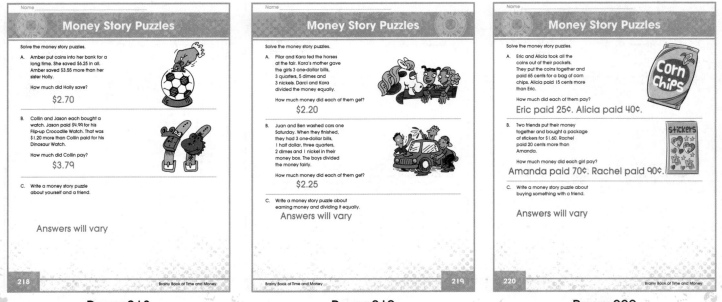

Money Story Puzzles

Solve the money story puzzles.

A. Amber put coins into her bank for a long time. She saved $6.25 in all. Amber saved $3.55 more than her sister Holly.

How much did Holly save?

$2.70

B. Collin and Jason each bought a watch. Jason paid $4.99 for his Flip-up Crocodile Watch. That was $1.20 more than Collin paid for his Dinosaur Watch.

How much did Collin pay?

$3.79

C. Write a money story puzzle about yourself and a friend.

Answers will vary

218   Brainy Book of Time and Money

Page 218

Money Story Puzzles

Solve the money story puzzles.

A. Pilar and Kara fed the horses at the fair. Kara's mother gave the girls 3 one-dollar bills, 3 quarters, 5 dimes and 3 nickels. Darci and Kara divided the money equally.

How much money did each of them get?

$2.20

B. Juan and Ben washed cars one Saturday. When they finished, they had 3 one-dollar bills, 1 half dollar, three quarters, 2 dimes and 1 nickel in their money box. The boys divided the money fairly.

How much money did each of them get?

$2.25

C. Write a money story puzzle about earning money and dividing it equally.

Answers will vary

Brainy Book of Time and Money   219

Page 219

Money Story Puzzles

Solve the money story puzzles.

A. Eric and Alicia took all the coins out of their pockets. They put the coins together and paid 65 cents for a bag of corn chips. Alicia paid 15 cents more than Eric.

How much did each of them pay?

Eric paid 25¢. Alicia paid 40¢.

B. Two friends put their money together and bought a package of stickers for $1.60. Rachel paid 20 cents more than Amanda.

How much money did each girl pay?

Amanda paid 70¢. Rachel paid 90¢.

C. Write a money story puzzle about buying something with a friend.

Answers will vary

220   Brainy Book of Time and Money

Page 220